LOVE AND HATE
ON THE TENNIS COURT

Love and Hate on the Tennis Court

HOW HIDDEN EMOTIONS AFFECT YOUR GAME

Stanley H. Cath, M.D.
Alvin Kahn, M.D.
Nathan Cobb

CHARLES SCRIBNER'S SONS · New York

Library of Congress Cataloging in Publication Data

Cath, Stanley H
  Love and hate on the tennis court.

  Includes bibliographical references.
    1. Tennis—Psychological aspects.   I. Kahn, Alvin,
joint author.   II. Cobb, Nathan, joint author.   III. Title.
GV1002.9.P75C37   796.34′2′019   77-476
ISBN 0-684-14925-7

"A fluid treacherous game. Advantages so swiftly shifted. Love became hate."

—JOHN UPDIKE, *Couples*

"Let's face it, the game of tennis is mental."

—BILLIE JEAN KING

CONTENTS

INTRODUCTION

Just what the world needs: another tennis book.

During the summer of 1975, despite certain moral compunctions, the three of us very nearly organized a betting pool among our friends. The person who came closest to guessing the number of books that have been written about tennis would have won 100 free hours of therapy or 100 free hours of tennis lessons, whichever he or she needed most. The problem was that we kept finding new books, so we never knew the winning number ourselves. The pool was drowned by its own weight.

But let's say there are 512. Or 6,053. Or 73½ dozen. Anyway, *a lot*. A few of them even claim to deal with tennis "psychology." What this usually means, we soon found out, is tennis "strategy"—everything from disguising shots to getting a good night's sleep. Our favorite is the one that suggests readers gather pre-match information on opponents from newspapers, radio, magazines, and television. This is a good suggestion, and one you should follow the next time you're preparing to play Rod Laver or Chris Evert on your local courts. Other such books are usually no more than glib little volumes that suggest you psyche out your opponent by doing

such things as spraying his racquet strings with glue or inviting him to play doubles with a timber wolf as a partner.

But most tennis tomes are how-to manuals which completely ignore the emotional side of the sport, despite the fact
that everyone who has ever picked up a racquet seems to acknowledge tennis as a "psychological game." (In this sense the
books remind us of prescriptive sex manuals—long on technique and short on sensitivity.) On the other hand, maybe it's
just as well that they avoid such issues. Books about tennis
often try to answer the hacker's prayer for an instant cure,
and promising to repair someone's psyche for $6.95 and a few
hours of reading seems even more misleading than promising
to cure an erratic backhand for the same price.

So here's a promise: we make no promises.

In fact, we were even reluctant to tell you what you *might*
do to relieve what we will call *tennis tensions*. In the end,
however, we decided that we weren't likely to alter triple-
handedly the penchant that thirty-odd million tennis players
have for receiving advice. So we've concluded eight of the ten
chapters with a "Net Profit" section, each of which offers a
few tips based on the material covered in the preceding
pages. In addition, the final chapter of the book presents a
wiser psychological value system, while offering some pro-
posals to help you enjoy the game at last.

But the main purpose of *Love and Hate on the Tennis
Court* is descriptive. It reveals the emotions that turn up on
the tennis court. They include love and hate and what's in between. Emotions are not foreign bodies, but many are unconscious and subconscious. They contain potholes and pitfalls
which can disturb the way people play. The first trick is to
recognize them and then *perhaps* minimize their effects. But
change is a slow and difficult process. You may find—just as
you do after taking a tennis lesson—that reading the chapters
ahead will initially make your game worse. Like we said: no
promises.

This is intended to be a serious book, as befitting a work that we feel clarifies the importance of emotional factors in a popular sport. But it is also intended to be lighthearted enough to emphasize one of our basic premises: namely, that approximately 80 percent of the people playing this game are taking it as something other than a game. For the most part we have tried to write in nontechnical terms, believing that tennis players already have enough problems without having to learn a new vocabulary.

Most of the case studies throughout the book represent real people. Many of them were—or are—patients undergoing therapy. For obvious reasons their names and ages have been changed. A few are composites. But a serious effort has been made to retain the authentic framework of individual personalities by making the alterations as subtle and appropriate as possible.

Just how the three of us got into this is a question we have not yet been able to answer adequately when asked by wives, friends, and other tennis players. The answer that is probably most accurate is that we *are* tennis players, and we have each experienced love and hate on the tennis court more times than we care to remember. Stanley Cath and Alvin Kahn are also psychiatrists with private practices and have noticed that a remarkable number of their patients play tennis and are able to relate it to other facets of their lives. Nathan Cobb is a journalist who has repeatedly observed that people behave in strange ways when they play tennis.

Love and Hate was born when we decided that those 512 books (or 6,053 or 73½ dozen) really weren't saying much about tennis tensions. Our solution was to spend nearly a year meeting regularly, with Stan and Al talking into a tape recorder while Nathan asked them questions and later wrote the text. Much of what we describe is what goes wrong on the tennis court, and it may leave you wondering why you or anyone in his or her right mind would ever play such a game. Actually, we believe tennis is a potentially wonderful and exhilarating activity which can provide more enjoyment than anything we know. And that's something we *would* bet on.

We would also wager that the book could not have been written without the great help of Estelle Bond Guralnick. Special thanks also go to Claire Cath, Margery McLaughlin Cobb, Dr. Francis Low, Dr. Natalie Low, Dr. Robert Mehlman, Dr. Betty North, Dr. Norman Sherry, and Kathy Tenniken. And, of course, to the patients who contributed so willingly.

S.C.
A.K.
N.C.

LOVE AND HATE
ON THE TENNIS COURT

1

The Hidden Lure
of the Game

Case study: JOE, age 35

Joe played tennis off and on while growing up, but not particularly seriously or well. For one thing, he looked upon tennis as being socially beyond the means of his hard-working but rather passionless lower-class family. For another, he didn't really feel that he was athletically adept, although he was probably more so than his parents led him to believe. Joe was fairly well liked as he grew older, perhaps because he offended no one with his utter diffidence and control of his emotions. He went to college, majored in architecture, and eventually married Susan. She was an enormous prize for him, this girl from the right side of the tracks who was the heretofore unattainable model of WASPish status and cleanliness. Her family was wealthy, she had blond hair, and she played tennis.

For several years Susan tried hard to get Joe to play the game. He resisted, however, which was not only a link with his past feelings of ineptness but also consistent with his general pattern of passivity and vacillation. He was unable to commit himself, not only to tennis, but to almost anything. Besides, he retained strong feelings of inappropriateness on the court, as if he still didn't really belong there. He never found pleasure in the game, nor did he feel relaxed or refreshed afterward, as did Susan and so many of his friends. In time, unable to cope with his inertia and often depressive negativeness, Susan left him. Joe was shocked by this turn of events. He had not seen it coming, was totally unprepared for it, and responded—among other ways—by throwing himself into the game he had stood so firmly against: tennis.

Joe now plays tennis with a literal vengeance, sometimes four or five times a week. It is clear to us that he is using the game for something more than a mere athletic tune-up. He is obviously angry, as seen in the aggressiveness of his style of play. The sport is his method of getting revenge, a way to show Susan that he will now play for others what he would not play for her. More than that, though, it is clear that he is trying to recapture some part of the relationship with her by taking up the game she played so often and so well. His self-esteem has been badly damaged by losing this suburban supergirl he sought so long. He says that tennis gives him an opportunity to be with other people during a rough period in his life, but what he really means is that it gives him a chance to be with Susan, even though she is not actually there.

The key to Joe's recent tennis drive is the way he uses the game to bind up his human wounds and to avoid feeling the depth of his loss. Something has broken in his life, and he is struggling to repair it. Tennis is both a ritualized and a social game, and Joe badly needs its formal guidelines to structure and cement his contacts with other people. As we stated, though, the "other people" are still primarily Susan. In fact, we would add that when he hits a shot over the net he is not really looking for the ball to return. What he actually wants to come back is his wife.

In the beginning there was Humphrey Bogart. Yes, Bogey: so smug and so clean, asking "Tennis, anyone?" through glistening teeth while performing in *Swifty*, a play produced in 1922. How was he to know that five decades later America would get around to answering the question with such an affirmative shout that a San Francisco jeweler would seriously design a $1,500 tennis racquet that features its owner's name set in diamonds on an eighteen-carat-gold nameplate? [1] That such an item could exist is mute tribute to the so-called tennis boom, as well as to every newspaper headline writer who

[1] The jeweler's name is Sidney Mobell, and making such tennis racquets is only slightly less astonishing than actually selling seven of them between 1974 and 1976.

ever followed Bogart's lead and thereby scribbled "Tennis, everyone!" above a story on this phenomenon of the 1970s. If we are to believe the pollsters, something over thirty million Americans—about one in seven of us—now play tennis on at least an occasional basis. This is roughly six times the number who were playing the game a decade and a half ago, long before professionals began receiving their paychecks on top of the table instead of beneath it, and even longer before the game made its way into suburban tennis warehouses. For better or for worse, the game has supplanted golf of the 1950s and skiing of the 1960s as the country's "in" sport. It is a major topic of conversation in both board room and living room, enveloping partnerships and marriages in a mania of bright yellow balls skittering across a 78-by-36-foot chunk of turf which is manufactured by man, God, or a combination of both.

Travel with us for a moment to a red clay tennis court located in the White Mountains of New Hampshire. On one side of the net stands a woman whom we shall call Sarah. She is in her early thirties, is wearing a light blue tennis dress with matching earrings, and has hit few tennis balls in her life before this moment. On the other side of the net is a man we recognize as Rodney Laver. He is in his middle thirties, is wearing a green tennis shirt with white shorts, and is the first person to win $1 million playing tennis. Beneath the summer sun Rod is receiving $2,500 to instruct Sarah and fifty-five other people in the fine art of the game for five days, six hours a day. Under the same bright sky Sarah and her husband—Tom, a lawyer—have together paid $820 to learn various strokes from Laver and thirteen far lesser known teaching professionals. Sarah, we learn, is indeed a novice who has accompanied Tom to Rod's tennis camp [2] with the hope of

[2] This is one of several camps operated under the corporate name of Rod Laver Tennis Holidays. There are literally hundreds of similar camps across the United States.

catching up with her spouse's less-than-average game. Rod, we find out, views teaching people such as Sarah and Tom as a way to earn a good living from tennis while he decreases his amount of competitive play. As graceful Rod hits shots toward awkward Sarah on this particular morning, the scene clearly represents both sides of the tennis boom—buyer and seller. While the sport is still decidedly something less than a "poor man's game," all sorts of "buyers" are getting in on the act. They are bustling off to tennis camps or frantically dialing their local pros in search of lessons. They are finding public courts overcrowded and rushing to join climate-controlled indoor clubs. They are watching more and more tennis on television and hurrying to stores in order to imitate materially the stars they see. But the message they carry is far more than an economic one. For many people tennis has become a seemingly inexplicable gnawing at the innards which can only be satisfied by a topspin forehand or a backhand down the line.

But why tennis? If we listen to those journalists who so freely borrow Bogart's line, we are forced to read a continual barrage of pop sociological clichés intended to explain the sudden popularity of the game. First, these observers trot out Dr. Paul Dudley White (or—in apparent search of further charisma—John Fitzgerald Kennedy) and attribute part of the surge to the country's manic preoccupation with "physical fitness"—the desire to look healthy, to appear attractive, to seem slim, and to act young. Second, they cite the fact that today's "typical American," whoever that might be, has far more leisure time than was enjoyed by his or her parents. (Not to mention money: tennis *can* be played at little cost but frequently isn't.) Third, they talk about the game's increased status, opining that owning a tennis court has replaced possessing a swimming pool as a measure of one's social and cultural worth. Fourth, they point to "open tennis," which arrived in 1968 and led directly to increased television exposure of the professional game. And finally, we are told about the pace of tennis, so finely attuned to the high speed of the 1970s, wherein a game that can be squeezed into a lunch hour is so much more attractive than spending a long afternoon lazily tracking a little white ball across several acres of greenery while riding in a small electric car.

Hmmmm.

Well, maybe so. There's little doubt that all these reasons—particularly when taken together—explain part of the recent surge in tennis interest. If repetition were truth, we could stop right here, which is precisely where such discussions have usually ended. But we believe there are powerful *psychological* reasons why tennis is attractive. We feel that once you begin to look closely at the game—and at yourself as a player and as a person—you will begin to understand some of the underlying *emotional* and *behavioral* factors that draw you to the sport. Often, the game's allure has nothing to do with a player's simple taste for running around in the sun (or, increasingly, under fluorescent lights). Instead, motives are often found to be lurking in the back corners of the psyche, ever-present but ever-obscure. Remember Joe? Now meet Ted. He is single, in his mid-forties, and an executive in the entertainment industry. He has been playing tennis seriously for about a year now. When asked why he took up the game, Ted gives his conscious reasons, repeating many of the clichés he's heard from other people. He wants to keep in shape. He can play a fast game around dinnertime and is often able to knock off a set or two before going to work. This is standard motivational patter, all right, and passes unnoticed only until Ted begins to talk more about himself than his tennis.

"In my job . . . well, my job is pretty chaotic, you know? Look at this. You see these slips of paper in my pocket? These are notes to myself, little reminders. My business consists of a million details, a million little scraps of paper. Calls to agents. Gross receipts. Record album sales. It's a hundred things going around in my brain at once, even when I'm asleep. And, to tell the truth, I'm not organized at all. Sometimes I pull slips out of my pocket that have been in there for weeks. Weeks! And I forget to call people, and miss appointments. My business partner . . . now, my business partner is just the opposite. He's punctual. He's neat. He remembers everything. He's organized. I'd really like to be like that, but I just don't seem to be able to. You should see his desk: nothing out of place, the pencils all sharpened. Then you should see mine: sometimes when the telephone rings, it actually stops before I can find it."

Question: Could it be that in taking up tennis, chaotic Ted has found the sporting equivalent of his business partner in much the same way marriage partners often choose opposites? Certainly he has chosen a game in which all the pencils are sharpened, a state of affairs he admires but has been unable to achieve. In fact, one thing tennis has always possessed is organization.[3] Originally played during the Middle Ages as "court tennis," the game was initially a hobby of the royal families of England and Europe. (Sometimes to their detriment: in 1316 Louis X of France died of a chill contracted while playing an early version of tennis.) It later became a pastime for other persons with a high stake in formality. Even when it was eventually passed on to players of lesser means after making its way from Britain to Staten Island via Bermuda in 1874, lawn tennis didn't exactly fall into the hands of the disheveled hoi polloi on this side of the Atlantic. Many of its early standards (including the wearing of "whites" to hide perspiration) remained. Despite the current claim that the traditions of tennis are breaking down in a fervor of "democracy" and multicolored hues, country club civility still remains firmly at its

[3] Yes, the game *itself* is well ordered. But this should not be confused with the politics of the professional side of the sport, which, as of this writing, appear to be founded upon the principle of continual and hopeless disarray.

core. The jungle shrieks uttered by the frothing followers of World Team Tennis have yet to make a serious dent in the prestige to be earned by sitting amid the cloistered courtesy of the gallery at Wimbledon.

Indeed, this civil game which once linked its players with nobility is still oozing *ritual*. And ritual is just the thing that would attract someone like Ted. Finding his pockets stuffed and his desk cluttered, Ted is in need of order, form, and stability. On the tennis court he has discovered a well-defined framework controlled by rigid rules. The lines are clearly drawn, and the ball must be placed within certain physical limits. In is in, out is out. Period.[4] There are also prescribed modes of action. Losers are expected to compliment their opponents gracefully, while winners must accept their victories by crediting them to anything from luck to the phases of the moon.

"Congratulations, Sheila, you were marvelous."

"Thanks, Marge. But you really had me going."

Now the truth of the matter is that Marge couldn't hit the ball into the ocean, right? A confrontation, however, would be unthinkable. Imagine this:

"Jesus Christ, Sheila, you were lucky."

"Go to hell, Marge. You know you stank."

It seldom happens that way, of course. Form prevails over substance. Style wins out over content. Thus, the kind of person we are most likely to meet at the local tennis club is one who is drawn—whether he or she knows it or not—to ritualistic civility. The tennis setting is one of order and regularity, creating a soothing arena which fills the needs of people such as Ted. And believe us when we say Ted is not unusual in displaying some of the characteristics of what is called an obsessive/compulsive personality. Ritual has been termed by

[4] Except when there is some doubt, disagreement, or even cheating. See Chapter 6.

psychoanalyst Erik H. Erikson [5] "an unexpected renewal of a recognizable order in potential chaos," a definition that could almost be transferred to the game of tennis itself. Think about it. Into lives filled with disorder and confusion comes this game in which people ask for something (a ball that has rolled onto an adjoining court) by saying "thank you" before the request has even been acknowledged! For Ted and most of the rest of us, such sanctioned ritualization subconsciously reduces anxiety. It removes the unknown. It makes us comfortable. No longer beset with uncertainty, we can approach the task at hand—namely, hitting the ball—secure in the knowledge that the only thing we really have to do to survive is to play by the rules and to be nice. Tennis is a sport in which there are many rewards beyond simply winning and losing, although winning *is* important. But what also matters, quite literally, is how you play the game.

Naturally, an attractive and important part of the ritual of tennis is the notion of being part of a group. And not just *any* group, for riffraff still need not apply. The game may no longer belong solely to the royal families, but it continues to maintain the aura of being a sport for the "right" kind of folks. The "right" kind of folks, after all, do not have arguments with one another over a point, do they? Instead, their behavior is subdued, reasoned, and polite. By playing tennis they become certified members of an exclusive club which is better and whiter than society as a whole. As The Thing To Do, tennis is a highly regarded social activity in which friends are expected to mix well. By definition, in fact, you are never alone in tennis; there is always someone on the other side of the net, a comrade who shares your attraction to the game's

[5] Erik Homburger Erikson came to the United States in 1933 at the age of thirty-one and became one of this country's most influential psychoanalysts. Although he has written in several areas of study, he is particularly known for his clinical work with children and for his theories of individual development as a series of critical stages.

rituals. And since the group sanctions the rituals, they become self-perpetuating.

Many tennis players create their own little rituals within the game. We see them all the time: the server who bounces the ball several times before tossing it into the air, or the receiver who twirls his or her racquet in steady anticipation.[6] Without such ceremonial activity on the court the player might become uncomfortable and even disoriented. When such regular formalities are practiced, the game is more likely to be wrapped in a warm blanket of agreeable familiarity.

Edna, for instance, is an advertising copywriter who is thirty-four years old and has been playing the game for several years.

"I know this may sound stupid, but when I'm waiting to serve and someone tosses the ball to me I absolutely must catch it on the fly. If I don't, I'm simply convinced that I'm not going to win that particular game. And, of course, I never do. I've actually skinned my knees diving after balls thrown in my direction. If I miss them, there's no way I can do well. I just know it."

In order to understand what is really happening to the likes of Ted and Edna on the court, however, we must delve into the deepest recesses of their pasts, beginning in infancy. Or, better yet, we should examine the backgrounds of all of us. Assuming that our attraction to an involvement in the rituals of tennis didn't arrive full-blown, where did it come from? Were certain people born with it? Yes and no, but birth is the best place to begin—or at least shortly thereafter, which is where many of the roots for praise or blame for the tennis boom can be found. In fact, we believe tennis mania can actu-

---

[6] A well-worn ritual on the professional tennis tour is the tendency of many players to wear the same outfit day after day if they are winning, hoping to continue their "lucky streak."

ally be traced to those moments when the maternal caretaker becomes the first object engaged by a baby's scanning eyes. (Sometimes a psychological cliché, perhaps, but nevertheless true in this case: it started with Mom.) While no one would be foolish enough to claim that this is the precise moment when one's fondness for the forehand motion is revealed, it is certainly the starting point for the beginnings of *play*. And, as simple as it may sound, play for most of us is what tennis is all about.

Ritualization seems to begin in the preverbal experience of infants and reaches its full height in elaborate public ceremonies. This suggests that the distance from playpen to baseline is shorter than you might think. Certain repetitive behavioral patterns begin as ritualized games during infancy, and it is during such games that you repeat these themes over and over again. You develop a certain personal coherency, a sense of style, and a pattern of relating to others. In time these themes become dominant in your life. In other words, they eventually become more than merely your potential. They become *you*.

It begins with visual play between parent and child. During the initial give and take of daily eye contact (which includes the child's learning to open his or her eyes in peekaboo style and therefore making things disappear and reappear) the parent develops a set of predictable responses, which in turn inspire repeat performances on the part of the offspring. One acts . . . then the other. Close your eyes . . . mother is gone. It goes on and on like this. Obviously, the child is learning something along the way—that the anxiety of separation can be controlled by mastering the knowledge that something can be brought back with the opening of an eye. After a while the child learns a new trick. He or she discovers that when an object such as a rattle is dropped, mother can make it magically return. Again, the responses are predictable on both sides. Such a game may continue for hours, a constant ritual of come and go. Clearly, this is a precursor of other childhood games. Hide-and-seek gives way to more physical and sophisticated games of catch-and-toss. Perhaps father makes a challenge of the game, tossing wide and high. In any case, a continuing variety of ball games is eventually played. Objects are *struck* and *returned*. Certain themes of behavior and personal interaction are being developed. Games such as tennis are not far behind.

Now listen to Norman, a journalist in his early thirties who played tennis when he was young, dropped the game for many years, and recently took it up again.

"After I started playing again, it took me less than a year or so to reach the point at which I'd played when I was a kid. I improved very quickly. Then I leveled off, which I guess is fairly normal. But one thing bothered me. In fact, it still bothers me. For the life of me, I can't learn to hit the ball from corner to corner. What I mean is that I always seem to want to hit the ball directly at my opponent. At first I thought it came from the way I warm up. I mean, during warm-ups you're not supposed to make the other person run. So, before a match I'd practice hitting slightly from side to side, and it worked pretty well. But as soon as the set started, I'd fall back into the habit of hitting directly to my opponent. I've thought about it a lot, and I don't know, I just feel more comfortable hitting to a spot where someone is standing, even if he's really a small target way over on one side of the court. I just don't seem to have any confidence in aiming for the open spaces."

What's troubling Norman? Perhaps it's connected to the reasons he took up tennis in the first place. In short, it's those old games coming back to haunt him. Just as he did when a child, he feels the need to *bond* with his playmate. He wants to interact—to fuse, actually—through the act of hitting a tennis ball back and forth. This is a strong tendency in all of us as we continually experience the need to relive the pleasurable moments of early play. Subconsciously at least, we are seeking the old activities that gave us hours of fascination and companionship as children. Making the ball go away and watching it come back—remember? It was a first skill and an early life theme, and it's almost impossible to put into storage. As we already pointed out, it becomes part of one's own style. Or, as Erikson wrote about the likes of Norman, as well as the rest of us: "I would postulate that in order to be truly adult, he must on each level renew some of the playfulness of childhood and some of the sportiveness of the young." Not surprisingly, then, here comes a perfect vehicle for satisfying that need for regeneration: tennis. It's the near-linear extension of early play. Norman's "problem" really isn't a problem at all; it's merely a subconscious return to the rigid give-and-take of childhood games. (It is, however, probably increased by the fact he gave up tennis for so many years—in that sense, he is still living in an earlier stage.) Norman *wants* that ball to come back, just as it always did, and he unknowingly makes the return shot easy for his "opponent." Conversely, other players may have difficulty because they expect opponents to bond with *them.* Like children at play, they wait for a direct return and are therefore frequently caught off guard. In the language of a teaching pro, it is said they don't "anticipate."

All games, of course, are extensions of early play. But what makes tennis unique in this regard is the interaction of its players on a one-to-one basis. (Except, of course, in doubles. See Chapter 8.) In tennis, whatever you do causes your opponent to react, and vice versa. A drop shot brings him to the net, a lob sends him back again. Actually, we feel it is often easy to predict some types of people who will take up tennis besides those who want order and ritual. One of the things some people also seem to want is more interaction and more feedback. They're people who are looking for self-expression and more human contact. Tennis is a game of psychological sharing. It is no accident that it is generally believed that the word *tennis* is derived from the French verb *tenez,* which means "you take it." Certainly, no team sport offers such a direct continual confrontation between individuals. True, the batter faces the pitcher in baseball, but not on equal terms: one is on offense, the other on defense. Most "individual" sports fall short as well. Golf, one of the most popular, involves a response by the player to an environment and to a score. Squash, the most similar to tennis, is not a purely direct confrontation, since it includes walls, which act as intermediaries. Perhaps the nonracquet game that comes closest to tennis—though without its physical demands—is chess. Here, as in tennis, there is an equality of roles similar to the parity found in early games between mother and child. A move on one side of the board induces a reaction from the other. There's no differentiation in status between players, no inherent aggressor and defender.

An important thing to remember about play of any sort, however, is that it should never get out of control. While it is a seemingly carefree exercise, it can end if there is too much freedom. The old adage is true: you must play by the rules. Without them there is chaos. And, as we pointed out earlier, one of the attractions of tennis is that it must be played within certain firm boundaries. The regulations of play are strict, as are the rules of behavior for players. We think, in fact, that one of the reasons tennis has boomed during the 1970s is that many people in the United States are yearning for what they see as traditional restraints and values. Having recoiled from the relative anarchy of the 1960s, with the alleged "counterculture" setting standards for social experimentation, that facet of the country we now call "Middle America" appears to be having its day and its way. And what better sport to represent these new feelings of conservatism than the most conservative game of all? Where else will you so quickly discover Erikson's "expected renewal of a recognizable order in potential chaos"?

Tennis, after all, came to America smack in the midst of the nation's frontier days. Its early popularity among certain families along the East Coast acted as a counterweight to the brawling lawlessness of the "Wild West." It gave the people "back east" a sense of tradition, a feeling that there was indeed an eye of order in the storm of madness. In much the same way, the first tennis boom took place during the Roaring Twenties. With the country rollicking along in speakeasies, and with organized crime apparently in charge of matters, players such as Bill Tilden and Helen Wills emerged to move tennis from a game of quaint gatherings in backyards to a sport of exciting competition in packed stadiums. Compared to an outside world deemed half crazy, tennis represented stability. Its values were easy to understand. It was clean and crisp and pure.

Today, in the same way, tennis is popular with many people because it provides limits to a society which no longer wants to tolerate open, frontier-style aggression, be it 1860s style or 1960s style. True, a tennis court allows you a great deal of movement and freedom of expression, but only within strictly prescribed limits. You retain the illusion of freedom but are really much more secure in the knowledge that the game will never let you go too far, that it will always keep you within bounds.

Witness the case of Shirley. She is forty-two years old, has two teen-age daughters (one who has just entered college), and is a "housewife." She began playing tennis five years ago.

"I guess I started playing for something to do, really. They'd just built a new indoor club in town, and some of my friends had joined. It seemed like a good idea, but, to be honest, I was pretty indifferent about the game at first. I stayed that way for a year or so, but then I began to get pretty serious about it. My daughters were getting older and were out on their own more, and pretty soon I was spending entire days at the club. I enrolled in clinics, and I took lessons, and I entered tournaments. I tried to get Ralph—my husband—to play, but he didn't seem interested. Oh, he comes down to the club every so often, but he doesn't take it very seriously. So I usually play during the day with friends. I have a lot of time with nothing to do and tennis seems like a good outlet. The house is empty almost all day, so why stay home? I'd like to get a job, especially when my younger daughter finishes high school and goes to college next year, but I haven't worked for almost twenty years and I don't know what I'd do. At the rate I'm going, maybe I could become a tennis pro, eh?"

Indeed, even though we haven't seen Shirley play, we can almost guess that she is on her way to becoming a decent tennis player. As you'll see in later chapters, tennis can be a surprisingly aggressive game. Although its boundaries normally require participants to keep their feelings under control, sometimes the rope snaps. In Shirley's case it has not— quite possibly because much of the frustration she feels toward her husband and toward the fact that she is finding herself increasingly alone in life is being relieved through firm overhead smashes. It may sound like a cliché, but tennis can offer a tremendous release after the classic "bad day at the office." On the other hand, pent-up hostility can get out of control. When it does, the ferocity that results often becomes so intense that it transcends the bounds of play. The result, as we've all seen, can be racquets flying overhead, balls careening toward fences, and curses filling the air. There is nothing quite like the tennis player gone amok, with his or her emotions laid completely bare in a game that stresses the well-dressed psyche. This type of behavior (given a certain blessing, incidentally, by the antics of more and more tournament professionals) is increasing along with the scope of the tennis boom itself. As we shall see, what happens between the white lines of a tennis court isn't simply a game anymore. It's a reflection of life.

SEVEN WAYS TO NET PROFIT

1. *Take an overall view of yourself on the court.* Before your next tennis game ask yourself why you're out there. For social reasons? Exercise? Try to sort out your motives. Look for the hidden reasons you're playing the game.

2. *Don't try to be a perfectionist.* Too much ritualization is inhibiting to improvement of skills. Remember that surprise is an important element of play. Loosen up. Take it easy.

3. *When losing, try a conscious change in set patterns as well as strategy.* There's no profit in being stuck in a losing mode, yet many players insist on sinking without even trying to make it to shore.

4. *Beware of making a ritual of the approach to the game.* Don't allow things such as what you wear or whether you acquire a lesson-perfect stroke to become more important than playing the game.

5. *Concentrate on hitting away from your opponent.* Too much sharing of play—or bonding—may make you a precise rallyer, but also a loser of points.

6. *Don't expect the ball to come directly to you.* Waiting for an opponent to play a sharing game is a good way to get caught flat-footed. Be mentally prepared to go after that shot.

7. *Avoid predictable patterns of play.* It's emotionally comforting to fall into a rigid and repetitious style which actually gives aid and comfort to the enemy. Instead, mix it up.

2

"I Thought This Was Supposed to Be Fun"

Case study: MARTHA, age 27

Martha did not play tennis as a young girl. Because her father was a career officer in the Air Force, her family moved from town to town and even country to country, seldom staying long enough in one place for Martha to develop a strong circle of friends. She was a better-than-average athlete in school—particularly at basketball—but participation in social sports such as tennis was limited because as soon as she began to work her way into a clique, it was time for her family to sell the house and move again. Her father was a muscular man who was fond of drinking and recounting his exploits during the Korean War. Her mother was more timid but felt strongly that her daughter should someday have a life that did not include changing locations "like gypsies." And placid Martha, unlike her friends, was not one to oppose a mother's wishes.

Not surprisingly, then, she has found such a life. After majoring in art history in college, she worked in the publicity department of a major museum for three years before marrying Mark, a successful corporate attorney. They met at one of the museum's previews, for which Mark had been a patron. He is fifteen years older than Martha, has two children who live with their mother, and owns a large house north of the city as well as a summer home at the seashore. It is precisely the kind of setting Martha's mother had always dreamed about, and the daughter has to admit that the thought of settling into this apparently stable atmosphere was one of the foremost reasons she decided to marry Mark. Her husband, meanwhile, is equally ready to acknowledge the fact that he was more than pleased to bring this young, attractive woman into what he called a town of "broads getting flabbier every day in every way."

Almost from the outset, however, Martha has been uncomfortable. Mark expected her to quit her job, which she did only too willingly, but this has left her alone during the day in a strange community among women who are for the most part a decade older than she. And then there is tennis. Almost everyone in the neighborhood belongs to the local tennis club, a venerable affair with an old wooden clubhouse and well-kept clay courts. Mark had suggested she take tennis lessons from the part-time pro, an aging gentleman well schooled in the basics. Finding that her athletic prowess hadn't deserted her, Martha became a better-than-average player within two years. She is known for her careful, precise, and accurate game. The other female members of the club have accepted her into their midst and regularly telephone to arrange doubles matches.

That's when the trouble begins. If they call on, say, a Wednesday to set up a game for Thursday, Martha finds that she is tense and irritable on Wednesday night. She often has difficulty sleeping. She wonders aloud if she is really up to playing these women for whom tennis has been a part of life for so many years. She can literally spend hours deciding which tennis outfit to wear. Sometimes her nervousness and anticipation become so intense that she has to call and cancel the match at the last minute, feigning illness. At other times, the sickness is not faked—she has been known to slip into the locker room to vomit before a game.

Prior to playing tennis, Martha had regularly managed to avoid competitive situations. Her mobile family life saw to that. An art history major, she did not find college particularly difficult or threatening. Her job at the museum had always been viewed as temporary. But this—this competitive community where her husband has put her on display and issued a challenge to the other women—is something else again. She feels intense stress when she's invited to play tennis. She believes she must play beautifully and look even better. Much of this pressure comes from the feeling that she must live up to Mark's expectations of her in order to hang onto the security he has provided. Usually the game works out well and she goes home greatly relieved. But it is the thought of competition and rivalry that is making her unhappy long before she ever sets a sneakered foot onto the clay court.

And so they are out there: hurling themselves into the tennis waters, cavorting in a sea of courts. Like thousands of fish that have been hooked with different lines, they are drawn by different lures. The bait can be a taste of status, organization, ritual, restraint, or the warm feeling that can come from the playing of games. The expertise needed to develop a well-placed slice serve or a sharp angle volley is not usually the concern of the novice, to whom such finer points are often initially no more than obscure references emitted by the television set on a Sunday afternoon. Such attempts at mastery will come soon enough (and bring with them a whole new set of problems), but the newcomer feels temporarily free to become immersed in such matters as whether or not to buy tennis shoes with leather uppers or the relative merits of the graphite racquet. As for learning the chipped backhand, that can wait for another day; right now it is time to ante up the court fees and envision a bronze suntan set off by white polyester.

The idea is to enjoy yourself. Supposedly.

For one thing, isn't tennis thought to be an escape without mystery or without threat, a replacing of responsibility with pleasure? What are we in this game for, anyway, if it isn't for fun? Think of the sociability that gushes over the courts in those good-timey television commercials that feature tennis.

"Wasn't that *fun?*"

"*Thanks!* That was really *great!*"

"Didn't we have some *fantastic* exchanges in that second set? Your gets were *sensational.*"

"And, boy, your backhand was *super* today. It was *beautiful.*"

"Thanks! What a *terrific* net hawk you turned out to be!"

Anything that is equal parts *fun, great, fantastic, sensational, super, beautiful,* and *terrific,* with half a dozen *thanks!* tossed in, can only have been made in heaven or on Madison Avenue. Unfortunately, history tells us that neither of these two forces had a hand in developing tennis. As a result, the game does not always live up to its press releases, at least psychologically speaking.

But hold on here. Isn't there the joy of what is called "body in space"? Doesn't this sensation start with some of those early childhood games, work its way through such later experiences as riding soaring amusement park rides, and culminate in the elegance of athletics? Certainly if you ski, skate, or swim, you must know that there are occasional and unpredictable moments when your physical flow takes you above life's tensions and you embark upon a sensual journey. For some reason everything just clicks, and you are on a kind of drugless high. When this happens in a tennis game, you can almost feel the sensation of traveling with the ball and sharing its impact. As Billie Jean King has said, "You get that esthetic value—that absolute thrill and sensation—from hitting the ball just right." [1]

Which may be well and good and accurate for King, who obviously experiences such moments more frequently than the rest of us. True, we all have our polite little conversations and pep talks after a particularly good tennis game, and we occasionally walk off the court in a state of pure euphoria. (Even if this is sometimes only because, as we shall see, no one has been embarrassed or slaughtered.) And there are indeed those divine split seconds when we hit the perfect shot and stand in a state of grace as the ball travels sharply away from a scurrying and befuddled opponent. But while tennis has ups which we imagine to be lifting us toward the

[1] *Newsweek,* June 26, 1972, p. 60.

sun, it also has downs which wash over us like thunder-showers.

Take Harold. A well-muscled financial analyst in his late thirties, Harold began playing tennis three years ago. Several of his business friends were into the game, which meant he would always have someone with whom to play. Since he had taken part in organized sports in high school, he was sure he'd have no problem playing the game well. Moreover, he thought it might provide the typical escape from the office and from the pressures of his heavy travel schedule. He invested $150 in equipment, became a member of a spiffy new indoor facility located in the next town, and mapped out a regular schedule that would allow him to play twice a week.

"At first, things went O.K., I guess. After all, I'm still in fairly good shape, and I was pretty sure I'd catch on. I was an all-conference high school shortstop, you know. And I had no trouble finding guys to play tennis with me, even though I was starting out. My problem was—is—that as soon as I make a mistake I start bitching and moaning to myself. I tell myself how awful I am and wonder out loud why the hell I can't straighten out. Really crass stuff. I honestly don't think it's a matter of winning or losing, but dammit, I feel stupid. Here I've spent this money on the game and some days I can't do a damn thing right. I get furious. I mean, how hard can it be for a guy like me to hit a simple forehand groundstroke? Anyway, all my crying began to get on people's nerves, I guess. There were times my doubles partner would tell me to just shut up, and one guy even came right out and told me he didn't want to play with me anymore. Said it ruined the game for him. But listen, I wasn't exactly having the time of my life either. I still play, and I think I've learned to control myself a little, but I know I'm not the life of the tennis party. I'm telling you, it's just so damned frustrating to make silly mistakes."

The next time you walk onto a tennis court, stop and listen to the sounds. Or, rather, to the lack of them. Sometimes the silence can be deafening. Why is there so little of the giddy laughter that is usually associated with games? Where are the whoops and the hollers? Why are people muttering to themselves under their breath, sputtering such things as "Oh, how *could* you?" or "What are you *doing?*" Now look around. Who are all those grim-faced people marching stoically about in white uniforms, giving the courts all the lightheartedness of a military field hospital? The game that was supposed to be a classic high (remember the television commercials?) suddenly appears to have all the characteristics of a classic low. Game? What game?

That's the irony of tennis. Folks who have taken it up as a form of relaxation often find out that it makes them tense. As an escape, it frequently works about as well as a jail cell. Attempts at mastery frequently end in frustration. Demoralization is likely to prevail. Not in everyone and not all the time, of course—Chris Evert has undoubtedly earned her title as "The Ice Maiden" and "Little Miss Cool." And an hour of well-played tennis by the run-of-the-mill club player has all the potential to transform the other twenty-three hours of the day into something positively cosmic. But for most of us there is that emotional coin-flip from the heads of pleasure to the tails of misery. A tennis game too often seems to contain all the enjoyment of being mugged.

What is seldom understood about tennis is the fact that not only are you playing against that person or team across the net, you are also playing against *yourself.* (Rod Laver: ". . . You really have two opponents: the other player and yourself. Most players have more trouble with themselves than they do with their opponents.") [2] Tennis creates intense emotional responses whereupon players quickly find themselves in a state of internal warfare. That is something you *can* hear:

Jeremy to Jeremy: "Hit the ball, you damn fool!"

[2] Rod Laver and Roy Emerson with Roy Tarshis, *Tennis for the Bloody Fun of It* (New York: Quadrangle, 1976), p. 125.

Mel to Mel: "That's right, you ass, hit the ball right into the net."

Jerri to Jerri: "Christ, girl, what did you do that for? How stupid can you be?"

If the game depended merely upon physical ability, you would not see or experience so many inexplicable breakdowns in performance which result in these fierce *inner dialogues*. No such luck. How many times, for example, have you walked on the court and hit sizzling shot after sizzling shot while warming up, only to see your efforts turn into dying quails when "real" play began? And what about the player who consistently manages to blow 5–2 leads, or for whom an advantage of 40–love is an invitation to lose three points in succession? [3] If success were only a matter of how well you hit the ball, such inconsistencies would be far less prevalent. But face it: you have days when you're "on" and days when you're "off," and more often than not they are the result of your emotions and anxieties. Your muscles do not forget how to hit a backhand, but an uneven state of mind can be as disastrous as not turning your shoulders.

As with Martha at the beginning of this chapter, it can be a mere request to play that sets off what we'd hereafter like to call *tennis tensions*. Even as the invited is hanging up the telephone, the psychological metronome is ticking away. Maybe the stomach is getting a bit queasy. At best there is probably a slight pause to calculate and measure the oppo-nent(s). There may be wonder-if-I'm-good-enough worries about embarrassment if the competition seems particularly overpowering. (There's nothing quite like an opponent whose service closely approximates a cannon to get the palms sweat-ing.) On the other hand, feelings of uneasiness and guilt may emerge in the form of gee-I've-already-beaten-her-three-times-this-month thoughts. In these and other cases, the spe-cific person who is going to be on the court with you can

[3] For an analysis of these and other familiar faces see Chapter 5.

cause tennis tensions. Depending on your relationship to your expected opponent (and/or partner), you are already worried about what kind of performance you will put on. The tennis tensions are off and running.

And who knows what will happen when the game begins? Alice, a forty-eight-year-old free-lance writer, can recall a particular on-court incident that went so completely against her approach to tennis in general that it psychologically destroyed her during the particular game at hand.

"I was playing with three other women friends with whom I've played several times. My partner and I were winning the first set, really playing quite well. We were ahead 4–1, I remember exactly. Sally was serving to us, when suddenly she walked furiously toward the opposite alley after a double fault. I could see she was upset with herself, so I called out something good-natured like 'Hang in there.' But then I noticed that she muttered something directly to Karen, her partner. And then Karen turned to me and said, 'The least you could have done is let her take an extra serve. You saw that she was bothered by the ball rolling over from the other court.' Well, of course, I didn't know any such thing because I didn't see any ball. And even if there was one, why did they get so worked up about it? Why didn't they just call a let instead of stomping all over the court and making nasty remarks. What are we out there for, to argue? I started to say something, but then I figured why bother. It really upset me to see them acting that way, even though I think it may have been because they were losing. But they didn't lose in the end. I completely fell apart. We lost, 6–4."

Obviously, all kinds of people play tennis. All shapes and all ages. And they each have certain clusters of personality traits which are in turn affected differently by certain external stresses. As a result, tennis tensions may well tend to be linked to particular reasons for taking up the game. Often when underlying expectations are trespassed upon during a match, as in the case of Alice, tennis tensions surface.

And take another look at Harold. Here is a highly success-ful businessman who is quick to point out that he feels he has retained his youthful shape and is able to maintain lots of friends. A sleek, good buddy, our Harold. He sees tennis as a chance to flex his still-young muscles and join in locker room banter. His self-image is one of perfect body-in-space mixed with a strong sense of masculine camaraderie. The problem is that none of it comes true. Harold gets out on the court and finds he can't master the game with his imagined perfect body. Balls zip past him before he can move. When he does make contact, the results are wholly unpredictable. Can this really be the Harold who was the hotshot high school short-stop? Not surprisingly, it isn't long before he begins to feel foolish and embarrassed. His tennis tensions rise. He begins a classic inner dialogue. It grows louder and more irritating to others. Harold's partners and opponents become distracted and upset by his behavior. He is no longer the good buddy they—and he—thought he was. So his tennis tensions rise even more. It may eventually come to pass that they reach a level at which Harold's $150 worth of equipment will be per-manently stored in the back of the closet.

Or consider Alice's experience again. As a self-employed person who must structure her own life, she has come to value organization. No one is looking over her shoulder. As we have seen, tennis is the perfect game for someone like Alice: it has definite form and shape, and it is particularly at-tractive to what is referred to as *obsessive/compulsive* person-alities. Among their needs are those for form and ritual. If the game is orderly, they are happy; if it is not, they become overly upset. Alice wants the game of tennis to go smoothly and civilly, knows that it should, and has in all likelihood chosen to play it for that reason. Now come Sally and Karen with their open rudeness and accusations. *Accusations of cheating*, for God's sake! In tennis! Suddenly the polite veneer of the game is stripped away, revealing raw inner feelings. Alice is uncomfortable. Her tennis tensions appear immediately. She fights back against her opponents' charge for a moment, but it is a halfhearted gesture that only makes her feel worse. It's just not her style to argue openly. She withdraws psychologically from the fray, completely confused. The shots that were so precise a moment ago are now uncertain. Her opponents, feeling comfortable enough to express their newfound aggression, move to the attack. Alice wilts, loses the match, and wanders away wondering what went wrong. "Sorry," she says to her opponents and partner, shrugging.

Sorry? Sorry for what? And to whom? Certainly not to Sally and Karen, who are probably only too happy to win a set that earlier appeared lost. *Sorry* must be the word most commonly heard on the tennis court, yet more often than not the apology is aimed at the self rather than the opponent or partner. It is often uttered because the downtrodden speaker is failing to live up to his or her own standards of play or sense of fairness. It's so easy to fantasize the perfect putaway, so pleasurable to imagine just how you're going to do it—and therefore all the more frustrating when reality arrives abruptly in the form of the ball settling squarely into the middle of the net. Every human being has an ideal tennis image on the court, and when the distance between that and what is *really happening* becomes too great, tennis tensions may crop up in the form of anger and shame.

What is really happening in Harold's case is obvious: his mastery of the game simply cannot yet match the image he holds of himself as a lithe, social animal whose body is oblivious to age. It's not that Harold is an egomaniac, for controlled exhibitionism and narcissism are healthy traits. Like the rest of us on the court, however, he is enraged by the difference between the real and the imagined self.

As for Alice, her tensions are not dissimilar to Harold's. Her self-image is that of a polite, demure woman who would never, *ever,* stoop to cheating or taking unfair advantage of another player. Even such a thinly veiled accusation—coming in an activity that mirrors her own sense of gentility—is simply too much to bear. Again, the difference between how she perceives herself and what is taking place is giving those tennis tensions their day on court.

Strangely, Harold may be in for even more difficulty in the future. Being a novice often allows one the quickly fleeting luxury of low personal-expectation levels. Unfortunately, should such naïveté exist in the first place, it usually doesn't last very long. As mastery increases, so do inner expectations. "Hell," mumbles the veteran tennis buff, "I've been playing this damn game for forty years. I *ought* to be able to do it right!" Unless this player begins to make some strides in recognizing and dealing with tennis tensions, they may well lead him or her around and around in a vicious circle: always trying to develop better shots and thereby increase pleasure, the player's increased ability leads to higher expectations and further tensions, which in turn lead back to the desire to develop better shots. Got it?

In fact, fear of failing to achieve an idealized self-image may be a major factor in limiting what has been repeatedly referred to as the "limitless" tennis boom. Many people who might otherwise be tempted enough by the status and companionship to go out and buy a flashy new racquet and a set of crisp whites are undoubtedly shunning the game because they already sense a threat to their needs for exhibitionism and triumph. They would rather limit their lives to areas of less risk than chance the naked truth on a stage that is so visibly located between those unyielding white lines.

But while the gentility and tradition of tennis cause it to be unforgiving, the speed and skill required should never be overlooked. Listen: tennis is simply more difficult than it looks.[4] The grace exhibited by a good player misleads the viewer into believing all he or she is watching is simplicity in

[4] If it were easy, why would the server be given *two* chances? And why do so many tennis instructors claim that the backhand is the easiest stroke to master, while at the same time advising you to serve to your *opponent's* backhand?

motion. The truth is that the rapid pace of the game makes it complicated. There is little time for intellectual reactions. In other words, who has time to think? Unlike chess, wherein moves and manipulations may be pondered for hours, tennis shots and decisions must be made in a matter of split seconds. This swift interchange of shots means equally swift disappointment. With the intellect playing second fiddle, coolheadedness is not likely to lead the band.

Margery is a twenty-eight-year-old graphic designer. She has been playing tennis for about a year and admits to not enjoying it very much. Actually, she has been able to pinpoint her tensions and anxieties and even to understand some of the reasons they exist. Why, then, is she seriously thinking of quitting?

"I guess I'm just not cut out for the game. I admit I let my emotions get the best of me. I know I'm a person who doesn't like to make errors. I've never liked being pushy. I'm a perfectionist and a peacemaker. The game just gets to me in a way that it doesn't seem to get to other people. God, I play this one girl who never bats an eyelash. Never opens her mouth, never gets upset, never minds killing you with her shots. Talk about your ice cubes. But I shouldn't put her down, of course, because that's the way to be. If you muff a shot, just shut up and play. Just pick up the ball, go back to the baseline, and serve. No complaints and no trying to dig a hole in the court with your racquet. Maybe I should take up croquet."

If misery indeed loves company, it is well suited to tennis. Margery's mistake is a common one: she thinks she's the sole inventor and proprietor of tennis tensions. But the reason there is probably not an unshakable zombie across the net from her is that the game of tennis and the process of life have an awful lot in common. What we mean is that *tennis style and life style are usually related.* Sometimes the connection is obvious: the player who successfully covers the court in short, constricted steps despite his or her seemingly awkward gait might well be a person who is rigidly self-controlled off the court, as well as dogged and persistent. Meanwhile, the player who seems rooted to one spot may be demonstrating a compliant streak. More often the relationship is obscure. Sometimes tennis amplifies traits that have been kept well hidden until the ball begins to bounce off gut or nylon. But make no mistake about it. You cannot escape yourself or the way you have been shaped by off-court images, ideas, and feelings. Tennis can be a miniature soap opera, complete with a plot in which dramatic turns one way or the other lead to a conclusion. Along the way its actors play on a stage that clearly reveals the way they handle the trials and tribulations of their lives. Do you fight harder when you're behind? Do you fall apart under pressure? Do you try to present an unruffled surface under all circumstances? What may take years to surface out there in the "real" world can be revealed in a few sets of tennis.

A classic example. In May 1973 a fifty-five-year-old former United States and Wimbledon singles champion by the name of Bobby Riggs played Australian star Margaret Court, age thirty, in a well-publicized match. Four months later, having easily disposed of Court, 6–2, 6–1, Riggs took on American ace Billie Jean King in a contest that was even more bally-hooed ("The Battle of the Sexes!" and so on). This time King was the easy winner, 6–4, 6–3, 6–3.

The difference between the outcome of the two matches was clearly not a result of Riggs's tennis ability, because on both occasions he played a baseline game dictated by his age and skill. The real keys were the very opposite tennis styles used by the two women, tactics that reflected their individual approaches to life. Court, a rather docile mother figure who has quit the professional tour three times in order to bear children, was simply unable to muster any aggression toward a male opponent. Her nickname is Mighty Mama, and the match was played, fittingly enough, on Mother's Day. (It is probably no accident that "love"—the holy grail in the worship of pleasurable emotions—means "nothing" in tennis.) [5] Court retreated to the baseline, where Riggs's lollipop shots could not possibly be cut off and were therefore more effective. King, on the other hand, is known as a combative feminist who has publicly admitted to having undergone an abortion, has led the fight for a separate female professional tennis tour, and has strong positive feelings about women in sports. She attacked Riggs relentlessly on the court, moving to the net to cut off his soft spins, making him run, and generally taking the role of the aggressor. Anyone viewing these matches did not have to be a psychiatrist to see that there are great psychological differences in the ways Margaret Court and Billie Jean King handled their respective contests with Riggs. And those differences were consistent with their life styles.

At other times even the surroundings can affect a performance. A stunning incidence of this occurred in two professional matches played in 1975 and 1976, both between Manuel Orantes of Spain and Jimmy Connors of the United States. The first was the men's singles final of the U.S. Open Championships played at Forest Hills in September 1975. The surface was clay and the surroundings sedate, just to Orantes's liking. He is soft-spoken and reserved, with a restrained and highly disciplined game to match. The Old World civility of Forest Hills suited him well, as did the soft courts. Although Connors was favored to win by people who refused to look beyond sheer physical ability, Orantes triumphed easily, 6–4, 6–3, 6–3. Five months later the two

---

[5] There have been several theories of the origin of the word *love* in tennis. One holds that the French, in playing court tennis, marked "no score" with a zero in the shape of an egg—*l'oeuf* in French. A more recent theory contends that "love" has literally meant "nothing" in English for some time, as in playing cards for "love" rather than money.

met in one of those "challenge match" media events, a well-publicized "Heavyweight Championship of Tennis." This time, though, it was Connors who felt comfortable. He is a brash and aggressive young player whose tennis game relies heavily on all-out, hit-or-miss ferocity. Now the setting was Las Vegas, steeped in glittering neon and new money. Like Connors himself, the environment was noisy and harsh. The indoor playing surface was not the soft, resilient clay it had been at Forest Hills, but firmer artificial turf. Not surprisingly, it was Orantes who was this time psychologically helpless against the onslaught. Connors won with almost embarrassingly little difficulty, 6–2, 6–1, 6–0.

Thus, tennis style can tell us something not only about life style, but also about how a person feels about himself and his surroundings at a particular moment. It can be affected by current relationships with relatives, friends, co-workers—anybody. Dan, for instance, is a doctor who has been on and off the courts for four decades. While it might appear that forty years of tennis would have sufficiently flattened out the peaks and valleys of his game, this is not the case. One particular incident stands out.

"Two years ago my wife decided to have an operation on her feet. To some degree she was having it done to please me—or at least to be with me more often, since she believed this foot condition kept her from playing tennis. Naturally, I encouraged her to have the operation. But then it didn't go well. In fact, I think I knew right after surgery that the condition might even be worse than before. Anyway, my tennis game went to hell. Really. I can remember standing in the shower after a particularly bad game one day and saying to myself, 'This damn thing has got me so upset it's affecting my game.' I knew what was happening, all right, but I didn't think there was much I could do about it. I was feeling bad because I'd told her to go ahead with the operation, and she was really only doing it because of me. It's only now that she's fully recovered. My game's gotten better, too, but I'm not sure which was cured first, her or it."

In other words, tennis can be a barometer of how you feel at a particular time about life and about yourself. Emotional hang-ups can and do alter the game. The results of psychological distractions can be as embarrassing as taking your eye off the ball and a whole lot more difficult to eliminate. If something in your life is unsettled—say, your job or your marital situation—your tennis playing is probably going to be equally inconsistent.

So what can you do about it? Is there some sort of mystical or magic high, a kind of fix to keep the tennis addict oblivious to outside problems? After all, tennis players frequently love ritual, and the practice of magic *is* ritual. However, if such a treatment were available, it would undoubtedly be advertised in the backs of tennis magazines along with the camps, vacations, ball preservers, and racquet stringers. It isn't. But that's not because there aren't any answers.

The aim is *integration*, defined by the American Psychiatric Association as "the useful organization and incorporation of both new and old data, experience and emotional capacities into the personality." [6] More simply, from our vantage point we'd like to refer to it as being "mentally together." On the tennis court this is somewhat analogous to organizing your body in order to make a good shot: you need proper preparation, footwork, backswing, contact, and followthrough. In the same way, your mind must organize and synthesize multiple factors—aggression, guilt, self-esteem, and various other things we'll discuss ahead. Integration does this by minimizing and containing all those extraneous emotional issues and conflicts that get in the way of play. People who are not integrated—both on the tennis court and off—will complain of "going to pieces" or "falling apart." [7] Conversely, when you're

[6] *A Psychiatric Glossary—The Meaning of Terms Frequently Used in Psychiatry,* 4th ed. (Washington, D.C.: American Psychiatric Association, 1975), p. 91.

[7] Paradoxically, however, some people who are poorly integrated off the court are at their best with a tennis racquet in their hands.

mentally together you often say you "feel like yourself." You're able to focus on the task at hand and to accomplish your goals. You no longer think about what you're doing; you just *do* it.

But nobody achieves integration all the time. If you take a tennis lesson, for example, be prepared for a period of disintegration immediately following the instruction. More than likely, you'll blunder around the court in a state of physical and mental awkwardness until both body and soul absorb the new material. More often than not, improvement seems transitory, for although changes may be incorporated into your game, many of the benefits seem lost as old bad habits recur. And disintegration, as we have seen, can come from all manner of outside stresses that are all but unavoidable. The trick is to recognize these periods of "falling apart" and to learn to tolerate them without being hard on yourself; it is also to strive toward losing your self-consciousness, to put aside the trivia of life, and to let yourself *play*. Tennis is still supposed to be a game, regardless of all those tight-lipped and stiff-legged figures parading around the courts.

SEVEN WAYS TO NET PROFIT

1. *Accept a basic fact: if something in your life is unsettled, it may unsettle your tennis game.* This is perfectly normal. There may be problems with your job, for example. Or an uncomfortable domestic situation. Or you may simply be experiencing a few of those indefinable blahs which sometimes appear out of the blue and cover you with gray clouds.

2. *Actually, there might be some days when it is best to admit that it just isn't a good time to play tennis.* On one hand, the game can act as a tremendous release for pressures and frustrations. On the other, there may be moments when you are able to sense that your personal emotional situation is such that it will have a negative effect on your game. In that case, it could be worth waiting a few days before you play.

3. *During a game take an occasional moment to step back behind the emotional baseline and tell yourself to relax.* Keep your emotional feet planted firmly on the ground. Be objective, and don't be afraid to face the situation with a sense of humor. Really now, is missing that approach shot necessarily as calamitous as a death in the family?

4. *Don't waste your emotions arguing over the score or line calls.* These are just the kind of extraneous factors that can take your mind off hitting the ball and concern it with things far less important at the moment. Once you start thinking about something other than the ball, be prepared to begin making errors.

5. *Always try to forget the last point, win or lose.* Don't play it over in your mind. It's gone. One of the wonderful things about tennis is the fact you start all over again, every minute or so. You have a clean slate after every point. If you begin to play lost points again mentally, you are immediately giving your opponent an upper hand he or she hasn't earned.

6. *Play with and against as many different people as possible.* This will not only teach you to respond to different types of tennis styles, but will also help you find people with whom you form a harmonious psychological "fit." There can be a sense of being mentally as well as physically "right," of being emotionally comfortable on the court with a particular opponent or partner. At other times players will find that they grate against one another. That is when they would be better off searching for someone else with whom to play.

7. *For some players it might be a good idea to sit down after a game and replay the psyche as well as the big points.* In other words, talk about your tennis tensions and the inner conflicts that accompanied you to a particular match. Admittedly, this type of introspection isn't for everyone, but those who try it might find that it explains why all those damn passing shots wouldn't even go so far as to pass the net cord.

3

Smash and Oversmash

Lou has played tennis since he was eight years old. His father was an excellent amateur player who toured the United States and Europe, leaving the boy to live with his mother for long periods of time. They lived alone, his mother walking him three blocks to school every day. When he came home in the afternoon he often played with the model tanks and armored military trucks his father usually brought him when he returned from his trips. The boy imagined himself to be a tank commander and fought violent miniature battles for hours on the living room rug while his mother made dinner for the two of them. But when his father brought him an English tennis racquet, the new game quickly vied for equality with the old. In fact, the more his mother took him to the local courts, the more tennis seemed to win the war with the tanks.

At college Lou became a very good tennis player, known more for finesse than for power. He played number-one singles and lost only one match during his junior and senior years. After graduation he, too, became a touring player for a while, following in his father's footsteps. (The older man had since died. Lou had not attended his funeral.) Although he never won even a minor tournament, the competition improved his game to the point that even today, almost fifteen years later, he is a top local player—which is particularly remarkable considering the physical handicap he has had to overcome.

Five years ago Lou was in an automobile accident in which the driver of the other car was clearly negligent. Several bones were badly broken in Lou's left arm, and he lost partial use of the limb. Since he is a right-handed tennis player, the injury hindered only his serve. And by working hard he developed an unorthodox toss which allowed him to compensate for the disability. Thus, the effects of his ordeal were practically unnoticeable as far as his tennis was concerned. But he never forgot the accident or the driver who caused it. The lawsuit he eventually won did little to alleviate the bitterness he keeps hidden beneath his success as a lawyer, a husband, and the father of three children.

Since recovering from the accident, Lou has become known as an almost vicious tennis player. His serve has a devastating kick, and he follows it to the net on even the slowest surfaces. Once a more patient player, he now goes for the quick kill with volleys that are murderously certain. This aggressive image is in total opposition to the one he conveys as a decent and loving family man, but it is not surprising. Filled with vengeance toward his absent father and the man who nearly tore off his arm, Lou is acting out his aggressive impulses on the tennis court. It is a place where he can be hostile, yet not cause any real damage. As long as his aggression doesn't interfere with his concentration—and so far it hasn't, perhaps because he is so well trained and experienced—Lou can use his repressed rage to his advantage. He has found that he becomes restless if he goes more than a week without playing tennis. He has also noticed that an hour on the court gives him much the same pleasure as did the afternoons spent hurling toy tanks across the living room floor when he was a young boy.

Lou is holding things together. He's well integrated. But many others are not so lucky. They're "falling apart." Psychological disintegration is an affliction known and feared by hacker and professional alike. It looms in stark certainty on the horizon, the tennis player's peculiar version of death and taxes. "Please don't let it happen today," he or she pleads. "Tomorrow, yes, but not today." And yet, unavoidable as it is, its symptoms often seem to appear out of nowhere, quickly turning the racquet into an awkward, flapping appendage with a mind of its own.

How often have you played a marvelous, almost extrater-
restrial set of tennis, hitting everything with a ferocity you
never thought you possessed—only to be brought back to
earth by the next set, during which your only consistent act
turned out to be swapping ends of the court between games?
Perhaps in the first set you were charging the net with abandon, pushing your astonished opponent backward with a
series of piercing volleys. But as soon as the following set
began, the net suddenly loomed larger and more distant, as if
surely your opposite number had mysteriously pulled it away
from you and raised it several feet. Your game "fell apart."
You were no longer integrated.

Or how about the player who easily takes that 5–2 lead,
and for whom grabbing the winning sixth game is only slightly
less difficult than trying to lasso a runaway rabbit? No matter
what is tried, games keep slipping away. The set is slowly
squandered, its dissipation accompanied by a feeling of inevi-
tability. "Here we go again," moans the fast-fading failure,
knowing only too well how frequently such self-sabotage has
happened before. In this case, disintegration is gradual. But it
is no less agonizing.

And what about the notorious big hitter who consistently
folds up when he comes up against an older opponent armed
with soft, lazy floaters? Present this boomer with a hard, flat
shot to lean his racquet into and he'll beat the air out of the
ball. But place a spindly-legged dispenser of rainbows across
the net from him and his zing is gone. The harder our slugger
tries to hit the ball, the worse he plays. In the meantime his
elderly opponent gingerly runs out the set with a variety of
powderpuff shots. The slammer departs the court determined
to increase the tension of his racquet strings. *Then,* he figures, he'll pummel the codger.

One of the most important psychological factors in tennis is
aggression—or, more specifically, how players come to grips
with it. There's nothing quite like difficulty in dealing with

aggression, whether it's your own or someone else's, for causing your tennis tensions to percolate on the court. But it's
vital to realize that when we speak of aggression we are not
talking about launching wholesale physical or verbal attacks
on your opponents or partners. (Though this has been known
to happen when aggression gets out of control. And in professional tennis, linesmen and umpires have become experts on
receiving overaggressive impulses.) What is meant is simply
the forceful action you must take in order to play. Put another
way, you can't play tennis without calling upon a certain
amount of aggression.

Obviously, the act of hitting the ball is an aggressive one.
All the physical steps of shot making—from turning the
shoulders to followthrough—surround a central split second
when the striking of an object takes place. "Do you want to go
out and have a hit?" is a common invitation to play tennis.

Probably more notable, however, is the aggression that is
generated toward the other side of the net. Tennis coaches
emphasize movements that thrust the player *forward.* The
knees should bend to launch the hitter onward as he or she
makes contact. The ball is best taken on the rise, rather than
as it falls. Players are taught—particularly when playing doubles—that whoever captures the net usually captures the
point. Conversely, actions that indicate retreat are frowned
upon. A "defensive lob" is intended as a temporary weapon
in the arsenal of shots, to be used only until one is able to return to the offense. Hitting the ball while leaning backward
severely limits power. No matter how good a player's baseline
game may be (Chris Evert is a good example), he or she is not
admired as much as the thunderous hitter who stalks the net.

Toni is a part-time clerk. She is thirty-two years old and has
been playing tennis since she graduated from high school.
She was single when she began to pursue the game and
picked up her racquet only about once a month. But unlike
many people for whom it becomes difficult to find time to

play as their lives become more filled, Toni has frequented
the courts more and more often since becoming a wife and
mother. Now she never plays less than once a week and
usually more often.

"I admit it. When I go out there on the court in the morning it's to
help me let things out. All kinds of things, but mostly just the hectic
life of trying to raise kids and hold down a job. I usually play with
the same people, and they say they can tell when I've had a tough
week because I run like crazy. The worse it's been, the harder I run.
For me, there's nothing quite like the feeling of smashing—and listen, I know just what I'm saying—of smashing that ball. For that
hour and a half, or however long it is, I can forget about all the crap
at home. I remember one particular day when I'd been up half the
night with my sick daughter and figured I'd never be able to drag
myself around the court. I was bushed. But, you know, it was amaz-
ing. I felt like I was going to drive that ball through the racquet. I
was hitting it so hard. In fact, I even broke a string. So how are you
going to figure it?"

How indeed? We've already seen how outside emotional
issues can have a negative effect on your game, and here
comes Toni with a story that seems to convey just the opposite. But it's important to realize that the relationship between life and tennis can work in strange ways. Aggression is
a form of psychobiologic energy which is probably innate in
humans, but it also arises as a response to frustration. It is a
perfectly natural and necessary human impulse. Historically,
certain games have been a major outlet for aggressive urges,
providing an arena where both participant and spectator may
sublimate such feelings. One of the major pitches from the
sellers of the tennis boom has been something along the lines
of "Tennis is a great way to get rid of your frustrations."
Which is true, because, as do all sports to one degree or
another, it legitimizes aggression. Play is *permission*.

When you begin to warm up before a tennis match, you

may shout across the net that you feel particularly "mean" today. But chances are your opponent will only smile. For while a certain amount of aggression is required to play tennis well, players are also mollified by their knowledge that no one is really going to get hurt. No matter how hard the ball is hit, a tennis court is considered a physically safe place to be. A heavy hitter may be joyfully termed a "killer," but such a presence is not felt to be a threat to life and limb. Another player may exhort his or her partner to "show no mercy" to their opponents, but this is not to be taken as a call to carnage. Being able to strike out at something or someone in this manner—*without guilt*—results in very positive feelings. Had Toni taken out her frustrations on her daughter, she would undoubtedly have felt an enormous sense of shame. But what's shameful about hitting a ball or forcing an opponent deep into the backcourt? Everybody's chummy on the tennis court, right?

That's because tennis, by its cordial and formal nature, normally limits or *binds* aggression. It channels it and thereby keeps it under control. By contrast, aggression in many other games is stark naked. But tennis is not a "contact sport," and you cannot vent your aggression through a crackback block or high sticking. The idea is not to knock down a row of wooden pins or hit a cowhide-covered ball as far as possible. It is a sport in which aggression is limited and matches the refinement and discipline of the game itself. Potential violence is controlled through gentility and ritual. Players are not to forget that they are still among the "right kind" of people. While they may oh-h-h and ah-h-h over a shot they find particularly "murderous," or even use a racquet threateningly dubbed "The Black Knight," [1] they know they remain protected by this most civilized game of all. When psychologist B. F. Skinner created a gentle utopia and called it *Walden Two*,

[1] This product is manufactured by Dura-Fiber, a division of Steiner American Corp., Carson City, Nevada.

the populace was encouraged to undertake only two competitive games: tennis and chess.[2]

The restraint begins even before the game itself. For instance, open challenges are not hurled at prospective opponents. Instead, queries about a game possibly being conveniently arranged are subtly posed. When the match begins, it is supposed to continue without argument or—God forbid—fighting. Passions are to be kept well in check. Debates over calls are minimized. (What other professional sport refuses to pay its officials, clinging instead to the notion that this is really a game for gentlemen and gentlewomen during which decisions affecting the outcome are really of little consequence?) Like the very rich with their money, tennis players are not supposed to let people know precisely how much is going on underneath. In some sports an injury to an opponent is looked on by the other side as a chance for victory; in tennis it can create an atmosphere of concern and even guilt at the opposite end of the court. At the completion of even the fiercest professional tennis matches, players are expected to march to the net with a fixed grin, shake hands, and cordially admit to something approaching eternal friendship and undying respect. In club tennis or on public courts aggression is to be left at courtside and not brought into the locker room. Tennis is viewed as a good "family" game in which you can be sure your children will not be injured. How could they be hurt by playing a game intended to be as refined as the strawberries in Devonshire cream served at Wimbledon?

By legitimizing aggression *within strict bounds*, tennis is not unlike an enormous sigh of relief. We all have pent-up anger seething inside us searching for an outlet. Sanctioned, repeated hitting can be a safety valve that releases repressed feelings of frustration and disappointment. "I feel better after I've played a good set of tennis" is the hacker's classic line, and most players indeed walk off the court feeling less anxious

[2] B. F. Skinner, *Walden Two* (New York: Macmillan, 1948).

than when they walked on. An aggressive offensive shot quickens the old footwork, and the orderly tennis setting allows it to be made without guilt.

Janet, for instance, has used tennis in two ways to bind aggression. Now a forty-five-year-old bank teller, she has been playing the game for more than thirty years. She began as a teen-ager and soon found that she was both literally and figuratively using tennis to get out of the house.

"In retrospect, it's easy to see the reasons I had for playing tennis. Whenever I became angry or enraged at home, I'd take my racquet and ball and go to a nearby building where there was a bare brick wall. Then I'd pound the ball at the wall as hard and as fast as I could. I even drew an imaginary net along the wall, and I'd go out after dinner and hit hundreds of balls 'over' it. Literally tore the covers off. I can tell you I developed the most fearsome forehand of any twelve-year-old girl you ever saw. Maybe my court tactics weren't too good, but I could hit the ball as hard as any boy my age. It was just a way to get away from home for a while, and my mother—my father was dead—seemed to think it was a good thing to do. Even after she died and I went to live with relatives, I found another place to hit. Today people ask me where I 'found' my forehand, and I tell them it's the result of slugging a punching bag. Which it is, sort of."

Kept under control, aggression in tennis can have a near healing effect. But there are also times when it can create definite problems on the court, depending on how much or how little is present (not to mention where it's directed). Let's start with the most obvious offender: the player who allows aggression to get completely out of control and whose presence in a tennis game is greeted with all the warmth that might be given the arrival of a poisonous snake. He represents what can go wrong with the complex formula for tennis Bill Tilden once expressed to his nephew: "You must have a killer instinct, even though you must also be a sportsman." [3]

[3] *Tennis*, July 1976, p. 76.

We've all seen or heard of this person, for whom the tight restraints of the game fail to work. The first sign of trouble with aggressive impulses is usually an extremely clamorous inner dialogue: "You fool,[4] Tom! You absolute, utter, and total fool! Learn to hit the ball right, will you? You're wasting your time out here! God damn you!" Because of the tight formality of tennis, it's common for aggression to be first turned inward in this manner. The player becomes openly hostile toward himself, criticizing his shots in a manner destined to lead straight to disintegration. It's only in rare cases that such self-flagellation leads to better play.

Even worse is your basic racquet thrower/ball kicker. By now growing frustrations are on the loose, and the player has decided to take them out on the inanimate symbols of his fruitless attempts. The racquet is scaled into the net or fence, the balls kicked toward the heavens or the ceiling. The inner dialogue breaks into open cursing, a near tantrum. Finally, if aggression gets completely out of hand, if all the constraints and barriers break down, physical violence may follow. It is the rare and ultimate final step, and one that is made even more horrifying by the supposedly enlightened atmosphere that grips the game. Open hostility in tennis sends a deathly silence across adjoining courts. It's as if a guest had appeared at a party dressed in a zebra suit when the invitation clearly specified white tie. People stop abruptly, take an embarrassed glance at the offender, and try not to look again. It is not unusual for such outbreaks to cause a plague of tennis tensions on all courts within sight and sound. If there is a tennis hell, it is reserved in the minds of players for what they see as these contemptible souls who have dared to express anger so openly.

The trouble is, few tennis buffs realize that problems with

[4] "Fool" and "stupid" are the two most prevalent self-descriptive utterances heard on the tennis court, nudging out "idiot," "ass," "jerk," and "dummy" for the top spot. One would think the game was played exclusively by morons.

too much aggression do not always turn up as mere fits of bad temper. Racquet-throwing scenes are the most visible and obvious part of the drama, but they are not the most prevalent. Far more frequent, for instance, is the doubles partner who insists on taking balls that could easily be handled by his or her partner. Or the player who suddenly releases pent-up aggression by trying to kill the ball, and while doing so forgets everything there is to forget about hitting a shot properly. Even without volleys crashing downward into the net or groundstrokes sailing beyond the far baseline, too much aggression on the court is seldom a comforting feeling. As soon as the player—trained always to be a "sportsman"—senses that he or she may have stretched the limits of the game's boundaries, *guilt* is the inevitable result. And woe be to the player who feels guilty, for he shall inherit all the lack of concentration and disintegration of the most outrageous racquet thrower. And in some cases it may not appear until several hours later.

What happened to Tim is a case in point. A better-than-average player in his late twenties with good velocity on his shots, Tim recently found himself feeling uncomfortable after one of his thrice-weekly doubles games.

"Actually, I thought I should have felt pretty good about what happened. I was hitting with lots of topspin and moving to the net well. We were winning easily. But I knew I was monopolizing the game to some degree, because I was intentionally covering more than half my court. It's not that my partner wasn't playing well—on the contrary, he wasn't missing many balls either—but I just felt I could hit anything that came over the net. So I did. Also, when we'd get up to the net for some close-in volleying, I realized I was trying to hit balls right at my opponents rather than past them. I was targeting them, all right, and I'm not sure they didn't sense it. After we played I had several drinks, trying to calm myself down. Later that night I had trouble sleeping."

The threshold beyond which too much aggression becomes harmful is different for different players. For some, such as Lou at the beginning of this chapter, the tennis court may actually be the sole province in which they feel comfortable smashing anything or anybody, and their friends are startled to find such storms raging within what they thought were calm personal waters. Since tennis style and life style are usually related, a Caspar Milquetoast is not supposed to rush the net with blood in his eye. Yet it happens, because he knows that the boundaries of the game won't let him go *too* far. In fact, he's one of the few players who realizes that tennis is really only a game.

Because tennis is a sport in which aggression is supposed to be limited, however, players are usually ashamed when it reaches unacceptable levels. Even if open hostilities don't make an appearance, the thought that one has been ignoble can be upsetting. The realization that you've been particularly ferocious in annihilating a weak opponent, for instance, may raise your level of guilt to the point where it affects your play. As a result, you may unintentionally "let up" during a game. Almost every tennis player has experienced those mysterious incidents when a winning style has suddenly disappeared without a trace. After capturing a set or two with ease, the player discovers that shots that were catching the line a few moments ago are now flying out. If these turnabouts happen repeatedly, they may mean the player has an unconscious urge to let his opponent equalize matters. The desire to even things up reinforces one's self-image as a good sport and non-aggressor—or at least as someone for whom aggression must be under control.

In fact, *inhibition of aggression* is more closely connected to tennis tensions than is aggression gone amok. Sudden flare-ups do the game no good, and impulsive gestures aimed at the ball usually result in wild shots, but they are not as common as simple fears of being aggressive. As we've seen, a certain level of aggression must be achieved in order to play the game, and a higher plateau must be reached for the player to perform really well. The shrinkers and the wilters can survive on the courts, but it is the hitters and the strokers who are winners.

And yet, many tennis players have difficulty finding the amount of aggression necessary to play a good game of tennis. Some harbor few aggressive impulses at all, while others simply can't muster what they have. Their problem isn't really hitting the ball at someone; it's more not *wanting* to hit the ball at someone. One of the factors that make inhibited aggression so complex is the fact that it frequently depends on relationships between particular players—husband/wife, employer/employee, brother/sister, and so on.

It would be impossible to analyze all these potential difficulties, but one of the more common is exhibited by Jon, an intense but excellent young player who has won several tournaments on a local level. Something of a tennis prodigy, Jon grew into a top high school player and captained his college team. He now has a part-time job which allows him to play every day. In fact, he still hopes to become a playing professional.

"Well, it's a very funny thing. There is almost nobody in my area whom I can't beat except my coach. The reason I say it's funny is because if you saw us both play you'd wonder why in hell I don't mop up the court with him. For one thing, he's almost thirty years older than I am. He's been my coach since the very beginning, which goes all the way back to when I was seven years old. My mother used to drive me to the courts, and he'd be waiting there rain or shine, ready to put me through my paces. I don't know how many hours we put in together, but I do know I saw a lot more of him than I saw of my father. Even in college I used to come home every weekend for lessons. Half the time he didn't even charge me for them. He's a fair player, and a helluva coach, but there's no way

I shouldn't beat him. He laughs and says it's because he knows all my weaknesses, and maybe that's true. If anyone does, he does."

Chances are it's more than that. Many of the world's top pros can't beat their lifelong coaches. More than likely, it's a matter of guilt. The coach has spent year after year as a father figure, molding the young player (son) into a superb athlete. Faced with the need to muster aggression against a person so respected, the player discovers he simply can't do it. In the same way, many club players find that there are particular people whom they just can't seem to beat, regardless of apparent ability. The motive may be obvious, such as a son playing a father or a young woman playing an older woman. More often, though, the reasons are submerged below the surface of the relationship, fermenting in a mix of guilt and shame over aggressive impulses.

The form these inhibitions take may appear to be purely physical. Failure to hit the ball firmly, for example. Or to take a full backswing or followthrough. Or to rush the net. Or to grip the racquet tightly. The tendency then might be to trot out for a few lessons with the nearest pro, believe the cure has been taken, and later discover that the symptoms persist. More subtly, inhibitions can turn up in the form of not being able to *win*. There is nothing more frustrating than playing well enough to emerge victorious yet finding yourself hopelessly behind. That's when you start blaming defeat on everything from the weather to your shoelaces, while cursing fate and anything else that is handy for turning your well-hit shots into continual losers.

And don't overlook the possibility of feeling uneasy about *receiving* aggression. Within the concept of tennis-as-a-reflection-of-life, this may frequently happen to the type of person to whom a small argument is a signal to retreat. On the tennis court his game is likely to collapse when confronted by a heavy hitter, particularly one who has a powerful serve. He

might stand at the baseline as these crackling shots are practiced, muttering, "I'll never get it back." Such a player may
be particularly intimidated when his opponent rushes the net,
finding himself frantically unable to choose between a delicate
lob or a firm passing shot. Usually, the result is something in
between, as well as a lost point.

TEN WAYS TO NET PROFIT

1. *Don't try to kill the ball—or anything else, for that matter.*
Tennis instructors are forever telling students not to "overswing,"
but they seldom explain why. The answer is that rage tends to make
you lose your sense of finesse and style. In short, it makes you
forget what you've learned. The expression "blind rage" wasn't
coined without reason.

2. *If you feel rage building up inside you, take a short break.* Go
for a walk around the baseline. Take a stroll to the net. Stop to tie
your shoe. Towel off. *Anything.* Very few people play well when
they're angry, and sometimes a cooling-down period can save the
match for you. Chances are your opponent won't mind such an in-
terlude, because your behavior probably isn't helping his game, either.

3. *If your opponent loses his or her cool, don't get overheated
yourself.* Open rage on the tennis court has a strange capacity for
provoking disintegration in other people. If the person on the other
side of the net—or on another court—decides to use his or her
racquet as a javelin, do your best to ignore the display.

4. *Remember that white clothes don't make a pure soul.* Aggression is necessary to play tennis. Further, a certain amount of anger
must frequently be tolerated. The trick is to channel both of these
into the game, not into yourself. Grip your racquet tightly and hit
the ball on the rise. Try chewing gum if it seems to help. But remember: tennis is *hitting.* Accept that fact.

5. *Don't let up.* The tendency to ease up on an opponent when
you're ahead is a strong one. Give yourself (and your partner, in
doubles) permission to be aggressive. Tennis players have such lofty

opinions of themselves that they tend to feel guilty if they win by too much. Don't be afraid to think in terms of showing no mercy.

6. *Don't become so obsessed with style that you forget content.* Many players have hang-ups about hitting the ball *for real* as well as hitting it *straight away.* Form and technique are fine, but they are only means to an end. If winning points isn't important, why did someone go to all the trouble to invent a scoring system?

7. *Beware of false guilt.* Don't worry, it's highly unlikely that you'll ever hurt anyone on the tennis court. In the sea of life's dangers tennis is an island of safety. Short of an occasional and literal run-in with your doubles partner, a slight bruise from a misplaced overhead, a twisted ankle, or perhaps a touch of that infamous malady known as "tennis elbow," injuries on the tennis court are as rare as speechless politicians. Don't be afraid to play hard.

8. *Examine your game for inhibitions.* Use a friend as a psychological backboard. Go out and play a match, then discuss where your game looks inhibited. Are you hitting the ball hard enough? Hiding at the baseline? Hitting your shots too much toward the middle of the court? Your opponent may know more about your game than you do.

9. *Don't get trapped by midget/giant psychology.* Too many players are awed by the power they imagine to be possessed by an opponent. They see themselves as midgets, while people at the other end of the court appear to be giants. But there's more to tennis than a big serve, so don't be intimidated by facing one.

10. *Beware of people who will inhibit your aggression.* This is one of the factors behind the well-worn tennis philosophy that your game always goes downhill when you play your lessers. But beginners should also be aware of characters who moan and groan or are easily distressed. Shy away from them. Let them play with *each other*.

4

The Ego Factor

Case study: JACK, age 53

Jack began playing tennis shortly after he graduated from business school near the top of his class. It seemed strange, even to him, that he had not been a tennis player sooner. His family had certainly not been wealthy, but neither had they been poor. "Middle-middle-class" would have accurately described their circumstances. His father managed the local branch of a department-store chain, and his mother dedicated her life to her husband and to raising Jack and his two younger sisters. The boy did well in school, developed a large circle of friends, and eventually became class valedictorian. He found his studies easy, made good grades, and was accepted into an Ivy League university.

College was no more difficult. Jack was initiated into a fraternity and made Phi Beta Kappa. He was also particularly successful with several young women who visited the all-male campus on weekends. He didn't play sports extensively but was well built and attractive. Although his father had attended college and believed he had done reasonably well in life, it was evident the older man had a great deal of pride in what his only son had already accomplished. In fact, everyone seemed to say that Jack had a great future in the business world. And Jack himself, from his ivy tower, tended to agree with them.

After attending a prestigious business school, he took a job with a management consulting firm. He had been recruited heavily and had determined that this was a relatively new field that held great promise for the future. Since many of his company's clients were tennis fanatics, Jack naturally fell into the game. He became an extremely smooth and competent player who could be counted on to provide a steady and tactical style. As the years passed and Jack's career progressed upward, his tennis improved to the point where it took a very good player to beat him. He was a man who seemed to know all the angles, both on the court and off.

At the age of forty-two, and still single, Jack decided to form his own company. He felt confident. Although it wasn't to be a large organization, he believed it would be his last opportunity to do spectacularly well in terms of making money. A few of his business contacts were happy to supply the necessary capital, and for the first few years the venture appeared successful. But about five or six years ago, as the economy started to sag, so did Jack's business. Large companies were able to do all right, but the smaller ones such as Jack's were feeling the pinch. His commissions dropped. His small staff had to be trimmed. Jack began to brood, sometimes sitting in his office until late at night, wondering if he had made the right decision to go it alone a decade earlier. It had never been like Jack to second-guess his own decisions. He was now learning that things don't necessarily flow smoothly and that obstacles don't magically disappear.

Meanwhile, a strange thing was happening to his tennis game. Unlike his business, it had not really faltered. But even though its unpredictabilities were relatively rare, their presence caused Jack to begin losing his cool on the court. Old friends were surprised by these verbal outbursts because Jack had always been viewed as a man who could maintain his composure. But now, for some reason unknown to him, the slightest errors seemed magnified far beyond their importance earlier in his tennis life. A particularly bad shot, even if made while leading 40–love, was enough to cause him to storm about the court in a rage. Lately, such outbursts have caused him to lose his concentration and in turn to lose more points.

Jack is well aware of the fact that his behavior and attitude have changed on the tennis court. But right now, the way he sees it, he's got other things to worry about. The business still isn't doing well, and although it has shown signs of making a recovery, his backers remain none too pleased. In addition, his father is seriously ill, and Jack's setbacks have prevented the son from doing what he feels he should to make the old man more comfortable. What Jack doesn't realize is that what had happened to him on the tennis court is intimately connected to the "other things" that threaten his need for success in his midlife crisis—his increasing sense of failure and the developing rage that follows.

Locating that fine line between too much and too little aggression in tennis is no mean feat. The progression from rage to inhibition worms its way through the psyche, conjuring up a courtful of tennis tensions. They can flourish in different stages at different times, leaving the hapless player believing himself to be the victim of a complex plot intended to deprive him of anything faintly resembling pleasure. Frustrated by poor play on Monday, he may turn vicious and knock several balls toward the fence. Concerned about this open outburst on Wednesday, he tightens up to the point that little he hits goes over the net. Completely confused by Friday, he is not sure whether to let it all hang out or pack it all in. One thing of which he *is* certain, however, is that he is spending a lot of time and money and effort making himself unhappy. "Either this game is impossible to play," he concludes aloud while trying to recover under the shower after Friday's game, "or I'm a combination of a thorough klutz and a complete clod."

There they are again. The number of names that tennis players have at their disposal with which to belittle themselves is astounding. It sometimes seems that this is a nation containing 30 million masochists who view tennis as an updated version of the rack. What a contrast to those divine instants when one feels an enormous sense of well-being on the court. Even beyond the blissful physical high accompanying the pleasures of body in space, there are magic moments when the integrated mind and soaring body join together. Controlled aggression and sharpened skills combine to heal the wounded spirit. All over the world games are an antidote to the load of responsibilities carried around on slumping shoulders. For both players and audience they are a prescription for escape. Games are so important to us that we pay many of their players hundreds of thousands of dollars a year so that we may get vicarious satisfaction from their performances. (Tennis, of course, is the latest big-name sport to offer such substitute satisfaction.)

Yet things continue to go awry between the white lines. Aggression flies out of control or can't be mustered. Shots are wild or lack punch. As with Jack, tantrums and depression set in. What causes so much aggression and inhibition? Is it some mysterious force dropped on the tennis-playing populace by a deity who soundly disapproves of the game? Hardly. To reiterate: *"Tennis can be a barometer of how you feel at a particular moment about life and about yourself."* The two key words here are *about yourself.* Most people are sensitive about their *self-esteem,* which we can define as pride in one's own worth and performance. The major source of uncontrolled aggression or its inhibition in tennis is a series of assaults on this ego characteristic. In fact, we would suggest that self-esteem—and what can go wrong with it—is central to all the complex and often baffling emotions ranging from love to hate on the tennis court. Surcharges of aggression are particularly linked with the dissolution of the emotional glue that holds a person's ego together. If a few cracks are allowed to appear in the cohesion of self-esteem, the overflow of disappointment and frustration will fill the crevices and bring down even the sturdiest of psychological walls. Not to mention tennis games. Paradoxically, overinflation of the ego may be difficult to tolerate. Being king of the mountain creates royal anxieties of its own.

The fact that there's no place to hide makes problems of self-esteem particularly ornery on a tennis court. Humiliation comes frighteningly easy. Envision, if you will, those first few moments when you walk onto a court. Maybe you're in a place where you've never played before. ("These people are all pretty classy dressers.") Perhaps you've never seen your opponent play. ("Man, he's got big forearms.") Maybe you haven't played in two or three weeks. ("It feels awfully strange out here.") In tennis you're out there in the open. By yourself. Literally and figuratively almost naked. People on nearby courts can see you and may even stop to watch. Even if there's no one else around, there's always the presence of your opponent, whom you're likely to be trying to impress as well as beat. (Tennis is a constant form of "Show and Tell," with one of its goals being to impress other people at all times.) The thing you don't want to do on this center stage is lose control, yet threats to and excessive pandering of the ego will cause you to do just that. So it's not only the quality of your play that can make your self-image rattle and roll; it's also what's *said* by opponents and partners alike.[1]

More often than not, the blame for the seemingly inexplicable states of depression and bad play that turn up in the middle of a set can be laid squarely at the feet of lowered self-esteem.[2] Most players bring a high expectation of success onto the court, and bad play therefore results in a lowered sense of self-worth. As we've already suggested, fear of humiliation may even be preventing many people from coming onto the courts in the first place.

Regular players, too, often get psyched out before they begin. Cheryl is a fairly decent "B" player who visits the courts twice a week as if by medical appointment. Her Monday session is always a lesson, and on Thursday she plays a

---

[1] One of the frequent occasions when what is said can affect your game occurs during those moments when players pass each other at the net between games. See Chapter 9.

[2] The vast amount of self-esteem involved in tennis is indicated by the concern many players have with owning and caring for just the "right" equipment. Everything from the warm-up suit to the towels is selected to reflect the ideal imagined self. It's not unlike buying a new car.

game. All very organized and predictable—which is the way Cheryl likes things, but not always the way they work out.

"One Thursday not too long ago, I drove over to the courts early to sneak in an hour of practice. I found one of the kids who's always hanging around the place and started hitting with him. Everything was going beautifully. Lots of topsin and good pace. I was even running this kid a little bit; I could see he was perspiring and trying to catch his breath. I felt positively revved up by the time the regulars arrived for our match. I was all warmed up and ready to go. But then it happened. I didn't play badly at first—no better or worse than normal. But I had figured after hitting so well with this kid for an hour that it would sort of carry over into the game. I could just feel all that energy I'd built up sort of seeping out of me when I didn't play great. Like an innertube deflating. By the time we got to the end of the set I was playing badly. Very badly. And, of course, I was in a real blue funk, too."

In Chapter 2 we touched on the difference between your tennis image and what is really happening on the court. Or speaking a bit more technically, between your *ideal self* and your *actual self.* We explained briefly that when the distance between the two selves grows too wide, tennis tensions appear. Everyone has a vision of what he or she looks like playing tennis, but unfortunately it's none too accurate. Mastery and control can be an illusion.[3] When you discover the gulf between fantasy and reality, you need your entire storehouse of self-esteem to pull you through.

Return with us to that tennis camp in New Hampshire mentioned in Chapter 1. On a hot July morning Mike, the forty-two-year-old owner of a small construction company, is

[3] One of the great attractions of tennis is its seeming capacity to allow you to make superb shots just often enough to cause you to believe you should be able to make them all the time. If you made fewer, you'd give up. If you made more, you'd enjoy yourself.

out on the courts hoping to cure a chronically ill backhand. A young professional is explaining to Mike that he (Mike) leads the shot with his elbow, jutting it out and using it as a pivot so that only half his arm is being used. The instructor demonstrates how the shot should be made—from the shoulder, rather than the elbow, with the entire arm swinging. Mike pantomimes the pro's movements, and although he feels awkward he immediately senses he is making progress. Before long he imagines that he has copied the form of the stroke perfectly, and he believes he is hitting the ball in much the same manner as the young instructor. However, during the camp's afternoon videotaping session the televised truth comes out: Mike's elbow still flaps awkwardly like a broken wing, his shoulders are not turned enough, and he does not follow through properly. The fact is, Mike looks nothing like he had imagined. Instead, he looks like the forty-two-year-old owner of a small construction company. He watches the tape in disbelief and a state of depression, his shoulders sagging.[4]

Mike's pride in his own worth has been shaken by his loss of envisioned mastery and control. Whether or not he can overcome this conflict between his actual and ideal selves depends on what other good sources of self-esteem he has available to him—a supportive partner, a loving mate, money in the bank, and so on. If these sources are present and his sense of proportion is operating, he should be able to deal fairly easily with his letdown. But if they are not, his faltering backhand is only going to add to the droop of his psyche. In other words, if healthy pride and self-worth are intact, the pricks and barbs of outrageous tennis games can usually be endured. If feelings and memories aren't positive with regard

---

[4] A common error among many tennis players is to hit the ball when it is too close to their bodies, as Mike is doing. Often, this can be the result of not including the racquet in one's self-image—in other words, of thinking of the body and the racquet as separate items. Generally, this indicates a person who may be unable or unwilling to be flexible in his or her self-image.

to the self, however, troubles lie ahead. That's precisely what has gone wrong with Jack, the once successful but now failing businessman described at the beginning of this chapter.

To use a well-worn metaphor, self-esteem is like an automobile tire. It can survive its share of cuts and bruises, provided it has been well maintained. But everything is vulnerable to something, and if a nail is picked up a slow leak and eventual flat tire can temporarily render the car inoperable. If the ego picks up a nail during a tennis match the result of the game may well depend on its sturdiness. With too little or too much inflation the journey ahead will be precarious at best.

Obviously, the origins and sources of self-esteem are important. In order to explain one theory of its roots without providing a complete psychoanalytical treatise, allow us a technical aside. After a child is born, it spends approximately six months in a relative state of emotional fusion with its mother. The next one and one-half years are spent attempting to emerge from this union. From the child's point of view the earlier relationship is sensed as a cohesive, harmonious, and almost mystical union. The child views its mother as an extension of itself. In general, if its needs are provided for, a basic sense of trust is established. This is a warm and wonderful time.

But with progressive separation and individualization the child realizes more fully that it is indeed an entity apart from its mother. Others are now vying for her attention, including the father, thereby posing an obvious need to learn to share. If the child is able to make this transition comfortably—in other words, if it develops and can maintain a sense of self comparable to that felt during the state of the original union with its mother—intrusions by others are tolerable. A good sense of integrity, identity, and self-worth may evolve to carry the child to its next set of challenges. But if it has difficulty coming to grips with the state of separateness, problems with *envy* (of the father) and *rivalry* (with brothers and sisters) are more likely to arise. They are also likely to remain as forces complicating the gradual development of *integration.*

There are obviously hundreds of other factors that may go into building self-esteem in later years—peers, school, romantic relationships, family wealth, and the like. But to a great extent they depend on what happened earlier in the establishment of trust and individualism. To return to our analogy of vulnerability: if a new tire picks up a slow leak and is never patched properly, a flat is likely to occur somewhere down the road.

Sometimes the effects of assaults on the self-esteem are unmistakable. Shannon is a case in point. She is forty-five years old, the mother of three sons, and she plays tennis as often as she can. Which in her case means whenever her husband is out of town, but never when he's at home.

"The reason is simple: he's so critical of my game. He's played all his life, ever since he was a kid. I started playing, oh, seven or eight years ago. He wasn't too critical of me at the beginning, maybe because it was just the two of us on the court. But as I got a little better and we started to play doubles with other couples, he got worse. It seemed like every time we lost it was my fault. I'd get so nervous and upset I couldn't hit the ball. Now, I'd be the first to admit that I'm no Billie Jean King, but nobody is going to mistake my husband for Jimmy Connors, either. Things just got to the point where now I do everything I can to avoid playing mixed doubles. He travels a lot on business, and as soon as he's out the door I'm on the telephone trying to arrange a game. I'll play rain or shine, so long as he's not around to watch."

Whether blatant or not, pricks to the self-esteem invariably deflate the equilibrium. The result is often anxiety or depression. One typical instance might appear at the end of the set during which you ran hard, imagined you'd played well, and even won, 6–4. Your opponent, however, has other ideas.

"Boy," he says, "am I off today. I hope you'll forgive me. I really stink." [5] It's not terribly easy to feel good about yourself when you've just been informed that the only reason you won is that your opponent was handicapped by some ambiguous malady. *Woosh* goes the air from the tire of self-esteem. Anyone who can win a second set after such an affront has a well-inflated ego.

But the carrot-and-stick promise of mastery and control lingers. With it hovers the belief that you will somehow please yourself by achieving your ideal tennis image. And, of course, there are all those other folks you're trying to please, some of whom are forgotten but haunt the back corners of your memory bank (a doting mother, a father who never won a tournament himself) or are literally standing across the net or sitting in the gallery. Indeed, frequently it's believing that you've failed *others* that may cause your ego to tumble, leading to overaggression or inhibition.

Take, for example, what recently happened to Kurt. A retired electrical engineer who takes his tennis seriously, he found himself in one of those doubles matches during which everyone changes partners at the end of a set. For Kurt on this particular day such a rotation meant going from bad to worse.

"To say I played lousy would be an understatement. Couldn't hit a thing, not a damn thing. Didn't seem to know where the ball was going. No control at all. Felt out of sorts. Started out playing with Ed and lost, 6–3. Switched to Alex. Lost again, 6–2. Finally switched to the other Ed and lost, 6–1. I was the kiss of death, that's what I told them. Kept telling them over and over, 'You don't want to play with me on your side, I'm the kiss of death.' Whoever became my partner started playing as badly as me. Then as soon as he'd get somebody else as a partner, he'd play better. Alex was terrific, ex-

[5] Beware of this ploy, as it is another sometimes used as a bit of nifty gamesmanship. So nifty, in fact, that it should be outlawed on the tennis court. See Chapter 9.

cept for the set he played with me. Both Eds, too. The kiss of death, that's what I was."

Believing that you are turning the game into a nightmare for others is a devastating blow to the self-esteem. And calling oneself the "kiss of death" is a perfect example of how overly self-critical someone can become on a tennis court. As was probably the case with Kurt, such self-flagellation often leads to increased self-consciousness, further loss of self-control, and poorer play. (Notice the repetition of the word *self* here, as in Rod Laver's earlier claim that "more players have trouble with them*selves* than they do with their opponents.") In addition, the rage caused by failure and guilt may be turned inward where it causes inhibition.

But the ego—like a tire, again—can suffer from overinflation as well. Too grandiose a self-esteem can cause as much anxiety as one that is too depleted. Certain people have difficulty handling what they want once they finally get it. It doesn't matter whether it's a job promotion, a member of the opposite sex, or a sweet passing shot down the line. It's that extra injection of success into the self-esteem that is more than many people can handle. In other words, if admiration is pumped into certain egos that are already at their limits or frightened of success, whole structures can burst. Some people are simply beset by guilt if they do too well. Others become worried about being envied. Still others are afraid of causing humiliation. It's common to see these secret inner wrestling matches on the tennis courts, as players try to throttle their own glee at having achieved what they thought they were after all along.

Herb is a good example of someone who lets praise get the best of him. Having fought his way up from a childhood of poverty, parental battles, and physical timidity, he has achieved no small measure of business success at middle age. Although one might think that having slowly graduated from his father's grocery stand to a position as a top-notch whole-sale produce executive would have buoyed his self-esteem, this is not the case. His ego is the pasted-on variety, hardly the type that stems from a happy upbringing. As a result of its sensitivity, it can't stand too much expansion, off the tennis court or on.

"I play with this guy, Jack, who's one of these people who's always calling out 'good shot' every time I turn around. It's 'good shot' this, and 'good shot' that. I know it shouldn't, but it really annoys me. I can't bear it when he tells me I'm hitting particularly well. I feel very uncomfortable and squirmy. I know he's right, but why can't he leave me alone and just play the game? Frankly, sometimes I think he can tell that it bothers me, because he seems to do it more and more as he gets further and further behind. That's when it really burns me up. If I wanted to be paranoid, I'd say what he was really doing was ridiculing me rather than praising me. It's humiliating to feel so damn vulnerable on the court."

Unfortunately, tennis for many people becomes a major measure of their own worth as human beings. *My backhand stinks; therefore I stink.* An erratic volley is no longer simply an erratic volley; it is a reflection of its owner's value. An off day is no longer just an off day; it is indicative of some sort of internal failing. A lost set is no longer merely a lost set; it represents a flawed personality. This tendency turns tennis into a forum of life and death, and what more perfect locale for the person who for whatever reason views himself as the "kiss of death"?

Predicting failure. It's another of the results of low self-esteem. You hit a dangerously short lob and bleat a horrified "Oh oh!" as your opponent moves toward the net with eyes gleaming. Your shoulders slump, waiting for the kill. But no. You are saved. He smashes the ball downward into the net. Or perhaps his putaway is not a putaway at all, and you suddenly find yourself with a chance for salvation. Wrong again.

Having given up, you are not ready for his weak return, and you hit an even weaker one of your own. Your prediction of failure, rooted firmly in low ego esteem, has become a self-fulfilling prophecy.

Eileen is a case in point. She is a thirty-four-year-old housewife and mother who has been playing tennis for five years. Recently, she and her husband, Rick, signed up to play in a local mixed doubles tournament.

"We got to the club and were walking over to the courts for our match when we ran into a couple we know fairly well. They both seemed to laugh it up when they saw us and then said something like they wished us luck because they knew we'd need it. It turns out we'd drawn the tournament's top-seeded pair for our first match, and that was all I needed to hear. I ran over to check the draw. Sure enough, we were scheduled to play the top seeds in ten minutes. Ten minutes! Well, needless to say, I got worked up into a good lather. 'How can they do this to us?' I kept asking Rick. 'How can they?' He tried to calm me down by telling me that other people weren't invincible and that it was a chance for some really good tennis. But I walked onto the tennis court all doom and gloom and even greeted our opponents with the announcement that I was almost too upset to play. Sure enough, my nerves really got to me during the first few games. I made errors and was hitting cautiously. But then, slowly, it dawned on me that the shots coming from the other side of the net weren't all that magical. Sure, those guys were better than Rick and me, but we didn't do too badly once I got over my case of nerves. I realize we couldn't have beaten them no matter how well we played, but I know we could have given them a better game if I hadn't been thinking about failing at the beginning."

If one's ego isn't shored up, this lack of self-esteem can reveal itself through a variety of other tendencies. One involves an inclination to *envy* other people and what they're doing on other courts. This usually starts with visual eavesdropping. You know the symptoms: your eyes become locked in on what's happening on an adjoining court rather than your own. Perhaps it's a particularly good player who's caught your attention: "Hmmm, what a backhand." Or even an attractive one: "Hmmm, what a body." But while an awareness of what's going on around you is normal, and the desire to emulate top professionals may lead to improvement, constant preoccupation with others usually means undue envy. And too much envy means that the viewer, unable to live up to his or her idealized self-image, is vicariously seeking perfection through others. As soon as you feel your sense of mastery being eroded, your thoughts tend to wander from the game at hand. "How about paying attention to *this* match?" asks the unnerved opponent or partner, whose own self-esteem is now also being threatened by your neglect of his or her game.[6]

Envy often involves a kind of self-conscious magical wish to fuse with another person, actually to *become* him or her. Anyone with a high enough opinion of the self probably wouldn't be prone to such fanciful dreams. And envy is tricky. Not only does it come from low self-esteem; it also causes it. By wandering around staring at others, the player is both destroying his concentration and lowering his opinion of his ability. "Why can't I do that?" the brain is asking, convinced that fate has dealt a cruel blow because of some unfathomable crime or inadequacy. Getting caught up by the graceful appearance of the people on the next court is a dependable way to interrupt the integration needed to play the game well. And to send self-esteem cascading to even lower levels.

Rosemary, a psychologist who is nearing thirty years of age, has been taking lessons once a week since she began playing

[6] Envy doesn't necessarily involve only the game itself. You might, for example, envy someone's high-dollar equipment. Sometimes the off-court surroundings can induce envy. Players in private clubs tend to make newcomers feel ill at ease and envious. Even in familiar surroundings others may make you feel inadequate simply because, say, you missed yesterday's big television match. Tennis players are very good at inducing envy in other tennis players. Sometimes you'd think they practiced it.

tennis a year ago. But she's a voyeur, particularly when she finds herself playing a match next to the court where her coach is teaching someone else.

"First thing I do is size up who's taking the lesson. If it's a woman, I watch the way she strokes to see if she's at my level, and if she is—or maybe a little better—I find that I can't keep my eyes off that damn court. How's he teaching her? I want to check. Is he doing anything that might indicate that she's a lot better than I am? Does he seem to be enjoying giving her the lesson more? It's the craziest thing, because I don't give a damn about the coach. He's just a nice guy. But I know I want to see just how I stack up against her in his eyes. Isn't that maddening? I keep telling myself that one of these days I'm going to grow up."

Envy, you should understand, is often closely related to *illusion*. What looks like an acceptable groundstroke to you out of the corner of your frequently glancing eye may be secretly infuriating to the performer. Or that seemingly effortless forehand may involve more blood and sweat than is apparent. Even the man and woman romping through the air in what appears to be an erotic symphony may be at each other's throats by the conclusion of their game. Since most tennis players are struggling to achieve a higher than realizable image of themselves, visions of bliss being enjoyed by others are often inaccurate. But illusions and tennis players run around the courts hand in hand.

Rivalry is a close relative of envy, on the black sheep side of the family. Again, it bears a close connection to low self-esteem. But unlike the envious player, the rival has no wish to fuse with anyone or anything. On the contrary, he or she wants to bloody well *destroy* an opponent, and the sooner the better. Rivalry may be conceived as being far more destructive than envy. It is firmly entrenched in the unyielding need to be the very best player on the court, come hell or high water. It is not to be confused with *competition*, which includes respect for the existence and necessity of opponents. Competitors are out after a good time. Rivals are out after blood. Competition is an inherent part of tennis which confirms a player's own value. "If someone is playing against me I must be worth something." Rivalry is an attempt at all-out, total destruction executed with all the finesse of global warfare. For rivals, 6–3 is not a satisfactory win; 6–0 is required.

This is not to suggest that a certain amount of rivalry isn't expected or condoned in tennis. As with aggression, the game itself provides a safe place for rivalry. Its white lines are similar to the ropes of a boxing ring containing the bobbing fighters. But when rivalry becomes so strong that it turns into an end in itself, demanding the humiliation and annihilation of the person or pair across the net, tennis is a conflict that isn't much fun. It becomes an unholy crusade.

What happened to Bill's tennis game one day is typical of rivalry heralding a collapse. A twenty-one-year-old college student, Bill had returned home during Easter vacation to find himself playing tennis with a friend from his high school days.

"Chuck and I had been really good friends before college. We hung around together in school, took out the same girls, and played on the baseball team. In fact, he was the class president three years running, and I was the vice-president. We almost went to the state university together, but at the last minute he decided to go to Yale. Anyway, we got together to play tennis at Easter, and it turned out to be a real life-or-death struggle. The first couple of sets went back and forth, with nobody getting too far ahead. Each of us won a set, and we were both exhausted. My legs were getting cramps and I could see that Chuck's face was flushed. It was hot out, but I wasn't about to give up. I wanted to beat him. Badly. For some reason it was important to me. God, how we ran in that third set. We hardly spoke to each other at all. It was so even: 3–3, the last set, the sun beating down. And then all of a sudden, he won the next three games. Whammo. Just like that. I ran out of gas, I guess. Nothing I hit had any steam left on it. It must have been the heat that got me. I know I could have beaten him if it wasn't for the sun."

Sweet revenge. Or at least an attempt at it. Like many people who confront excessive rivalry, Bill apparently resigned completely. As can happen with too much aggression, guilt and inhibition set in. Concentration was affected. Or it can work another way, resulting in those banes of tennis, *bad losers* and *bad winners*. The bad winner is a giddy sort, gloating not from having lifted himself but from having put someone else down. The bad loser is the hopelessly distraught type, hating himself and his opponent while blaming defeat on the hot weather or the cold. (Now that so much tennis is played in air-conditioned surroundings, both excuses can be used year-round.)

And let us not forget *vanity*, whose name is superstar. Tennis, with its players and play so open to view, is a clear vanity meter. Watch it go up. How many times—*how many times?*—have you gone for the big, strong-armed putaway as soon as a demure young thing appeared on the next court? Or tried to impress the suntanned gentleman beyond the fence with your pirouettes in the forecourt? (Pirouettes in the forecourt?) Excessive pride in one's appearance or accomplishments is the hand that fits the tennis glove. It all goes back to the search for the ideal self, but in this case it grows into a desire for perfection and a wish to be the fairest of them all. The desire for mastery is one thing; the push for total power is another. Vain players are usually unable to tolerate imperfections of any sort in themselves. They are Greek gods hoping to reside in the State of Flawlessness, hot on the winged heels of omnipotence while dreaming of glory. Often they go for broke—meaning they attempt dramatic, sudden winners—with less than smashing results. Let the vain tennis player come up with a few badly played games early in a match and he may not recover. Reality usually wins the day, imposing its limitations on the deepest wishes for total mastery. The vain player, setting his or her sights so high, can usually expect repeated lows. And tennis tensions, too.

The circuitous route to tennis tensions is now complete. It begins at the beginning with a shaky opinion of one's own self-worth. Assaults on a self-esteem that is already low are the major reasons for the on-court overaggressor and his inhibited counterpart. The difference between the actual self (shot ballooning over the opposite baseline) and the ideal self (shot zipping down the line) leads straight to frustration and depression. As tennis becomes a life-or-death measure of one's value as a human being, it tugs players away from the relaxation it is supposed to provide and steers them sharply toward acute self-consciousness. Cool concentration may give way to hot impulsiveness. And in order to maintain mastery and control on the tennis court, you must relax and concentrate. *Control*—of the body, racquet, ball, and opponent. It is the light at the end of the tennis tunnel, reachable only if the player can crawl over tennis tensions that sometimes seem as big as boulders.

As for the reasons for low self-esteem . . . it's back to reading the "barometer of life." *If something in your life is unsettled, your tennis playing is probably going to be inconsistent.* For the most part, hang-ups on the tennis court reflect unsolved issues and relationships in the player's total existence. They continue to show up like old movies. The projector is turned on to reveal a business failure, a rocky love affair, a sick child. The ego may be affected by all sorts of memories and events—starting with that earliest mother/child relationship—and rises and falls accordingly as life progresses. The higher the level of self-esteem the better you are going to be able to tolerate a dreadful day (or week or year) on the court. Good self-esteem is closely related to good integration: a sense of being pulled together psychologically and of being able to accomplish what's ahead with minimal outside interference.

Yeah, you say. If it's so simple, what are all those people doing on the tennis court?

TEN WAYS TO NET PROFIT

1. *Don't interpret failing as a defect.* Regardless of what you may believe to the contrary, your life and times do not depend on whether or not you double fault. The game is simply not a measure of your worth as a human being. No game is.

2. *Expect frequent differences between the way you want to play and the way you actually do play.* Everyone has that picture of the ideal tennis self hanging over the mantelpiece of the mind. Fine. But don't expect to match it too often. Be ready for imperfections and limitations in your game. Lots of them.

3. *Don't predict failure.* If you're like the rest of us, it will arrive soon enough. No need to give it any help. If you send a fluttering lob toward the racquet of a waiting opponent, make sure he or she wins the point before you give it away. Or if someone walks on the court in a $75 warm-up suit, don't throw in the towel before getting your feet wet.

4. *Try not to worry about "ruining" the game for other people.* This is not an easy thing to do, particularly when playing doubles. But remember that you're probably not "ruining" the game for anyone but yourself. Other players usually have enough problems of their own to think about without being bothered by your misplays. If they don't, worrying about you is going to do their games more harm than will ever be caused by your errant shots.

5. *Stop staring at illusions of starring.* Often it's only your imagination, and it's a waste of time. Tennis players are forever attributing skills to other tennis players which are only illusionary. What looks to be a succession of perfect shots from someone else's racquet may be as infuriating to that person as are your own attempts to you.

6. *Be alert to other people's attempts to make you feel envious.* Tennis players are extremely polished at this. Name dropping, in

particular, is their specialty. They can tell you they've just bought the latest racquet from Sydney or spent the morning hitting with a combination of Ilie Nastase and Evonne Goolagong Cawley. So what?

7. *Leave excessive rivalry in the locker room.* If you feel you have to pulverize your opponent, many players won't want to have much to do with you. But look at it from another point of view: excessive rivalry often leads to massive feelings of guilt which may lead to inhibition. And inhibition won't help your game.

8. *Avoid becoming a bad winner. Not to mention a bad loser.* Gloating or fuming will not endear you to your opponents or partners. Don't exult in victory or cry in defeat. A good rule to remember: when in doubt, shut up.

9. *Ignore both criticisms and compliments until after the game.* Your self-esteem barometer is likely to fluctuate during a match, and it would be best to try to keep it at midpoint. Too little will lead to depression. Too much, particularly if you're subject to vanity, could lead straight to guilt and inhibition.

10. *Let yourself include the racquet as part of your body image.* Many players, particularly beginners, misjudge the distance between themselves and the ball. While this may appear to be a purely physical problem, it can sometimes be related to an unwillingness to adopt a flexible self-image. Think of the racquet as an extension of your arm.

5

Patty-cakers, Reluctant Smashers, and Other Court Characters

Ah yes, what about all those seemingly bizarre people you see on the tennis courts? The fact is, they may not be particularly bizarre at all. Despite your belief to the contrary, their behavior is usually not farfetched or unconventional. It's just that they don't play tennis in an emotional vacuum, any more than they do without strings on their racquets. Controlling your anxieties is one thing; eliminating them is something else. Completely turning off the emotional current in tennis is only slightly less difficult than locating an available public court at noon on the Saturday of the Fourth of July weekend.[1]

As we've indicated, a tennis court does not exactly provide a host of places to hide those quirky behavioral patterns. There stands the intrepid tennis player out in the middle of a desert consisting of one-sixteenth of an acre of high visibility, with his or her emotions and anxieties whirling around like a

[1] Certain professional tennis players claim that they are able to reach states of total concentration by shutting off their emotions. For them, this may indeed be possible. Despite this, they're no more capable than you are of locating an available public court at noon on the Saturday of the Fourth of July weekend.

72

windblown lob. Given such wide-open spaces, it's hardly surprising that questions of ritual, aggression, and self-esteem—which are intertwined like a three-ring pretzel—often result in appearances more akin to a three-ring circus. There are no opposing linebackers on whom to take out tennis tensions, no helmets to help muffle inner dialogues. Everything is open to sight and sound.

How well you can conjure up the familiar faces of the thirty-four examples ahead—each related to the ideas presented in the first four chapters and grouped here by emotional proximity to one another. They are among the ones you've come to love and hate on the tennis court. A few of them have been introduced already, but they have many companions. You may never have understood what makes them do such apparently "bizarre" things as continually attempting low-risk shots, habitually insisting upon knowing the location of all the balls, or consistently forgetting the score. What makes certain people chatter like macaws on the courts? Why are others always apologizing? Why is it that some players seem never to be able to finish off their opponents? Just as there is one right way to hit a forehand and fifty-seven certifiably wrong ways, so is the emotionally controlled player far outnumbered by his or her strained counterparts.

Naturally, it's a bit simplistic to say that A is always caused by B, particularly when dealing with emotions. Don't deduce, for example, that every patty-cake tennis player is suffering from inhibition of aggression or that every equipment freak is panting after the magical acquisition of strength and skill. What we've done is focus on one or two principal causes for certain types of familiar tennis faces, based on many hours spent professionally analyzing amateur tennis players.

And don't think that each player you meet (yourself included; is *either* a Doomsayer *or* a Continual Berater *or* the like. You might rightfully conclude, for example, that you're three parts Infinite Rallier, two parts Social Climber, and one part Commander-in-Chief with a dash of Reluctant Smasher tossed in. In any case, if you can't find something familiar among these thirty-four characters, you either (1) think "15–love" means group sex, (2) believe that Vitas Gerulaitis is similar to chicken pox, (3) are convinced that "metal racquet" refers to the United States steel industry, or (4) all of the above.

1. For whom the ball bounces. Again and again.

SYMPTOM: The player bounces the ball repeatedly before serving.

ANALYSIS: The world record for number of bounces before a serve remains unrecorded, though many tennis players swear they know it was set by a particular opponent on a particular day. In any case, the sometimes annoying practice (bothersome particularly to the person across the net) is tied to the obsesssive/compulsive person's need for the regularity and control he finds in *ritual.* Such fixed routines—called *obsessional mechanisms*—relieve anxiety by their very repetition. They offer the sense of control so necessary to make such civilized persons more comfortable. Bouncing the ball wards off bad luck in much the same way as does stepping over the cracks in the sidewalk. However, the former can be a lot more effective than crack jumping: ball bouncing may actually work, because the result is a lessening of anxieties. If you want to see a sudden case of tennis tensions break out on the court, inform a chronic ball bouncer that the United States Tennis Association has just passed a rule prohibiting the act. A nasty joke.

2. Out of sight doesn't necessarily mean out of mind.

SYMPTOM: The player insists on knowing where all three balls are located before he serves.

ANALYSIS: There's no use humorously trying to inform this player that ball manufacturers package balls in threes because they *expect* one to be lost. He won't laugh. In fact, if one ball is missing he may delay the game until it is found, no matter how long it takes. Like the ball bouncer, this player is heavily into a ritual of game playing: he wants the ball to return to him in much the same way things always reappeared during childhood games such as peekaboo or hide-and-seek. He is anxious about separation, and reassurance of contact with the ball is security: Linus and his blanket.

Further, displacing concerns about the *real* game with worries about the number of balls on the court means our player can concern himself with a relatively easy problem to solve. It's much simpler—and causes much less anxiety—to search for a ball rather than to deal with the issues of winning and losing.

3. Too much togetherness in tennis can lead to losing at love.

SYMPTOM: The player finds that he tends to hit the ball directly at his opponent rather than away, regardless of the attractive wide-open spaces that are available.

ANALYSIS: This familiar face turned up in Chapter 1, but it is so common that tennis players should commit its features to memory. Hitting *toward* an opponent is another example of reliving the pleasures of early play. Many childhood games involve the harmonious bonding of two people through an object that moves back and forth. It is extremely difficult for adults to kick this bonding habit. Such play was, after all, fun. When people get out on the tennis court, they tend to want to make the ball go directly back at their opponents—so that their opponents can in turn send it directly back to them. This little bit of togetherness may feel nice, but it's not the way the game is supposed to be played or won.

4. The Equipment Freak

SYMPTOM: The player has to have the latest composite racquet (to accompany the wood, aluminum, and fiber glass models with which he always appears on the court), the newest Italian tennis wear, a leather bag imported from Spain, and enough locker room deodorants and sprays to alter forever the human sense of smell.

ANALYSIS: As hinted in the last chapter, Equipment Freaks may have a flawed self-image which they're trying to cover with such items as tailored tennis outfits, while attempting to add to their sense of power by inducing envy and admiration in others. For these people, the "body ego" may desperately need a boost. More often than not, however, the new equipment will develop an imagined flaw or two of its own and will have to be replaced by still newer products.

The Equipment Freak may also be seeking a bit of *magic*. The notion of magic is partially what rituals are all about: the belief that something outside the game will miraculously alter an inferior style of play.[2] The more helpless you feel, the more likely you are to fall back on magical wishes to rescue you. Thus, an expensive new outfit becomes the latest sleight-of-hand attempt to get into the ideal game.

5. The Social Climber

SYMPTOM: The player isn't found on the courts as much as he is found in the locker room, the pro shop, or the bar.

ANALYSIS: Amateur baseball players do not make a big deal out of which playground they frequent, but most tennis players will be happy to remind you of which club(s) they belong to. As a game for the "right" kind of people, tennis provides a comfortable, ritualistic setting of the highest order. It enhances your self-esteem to be found in this world of literally white on white, where people mingle in apparent civilized camaraderie while chatting in muffled voices. Belonging to any group is gratifying, but hanging out with *these* people is downright intoxicating. Who needs to venture more than occasionally onto the court—where you get all sweaty and run

[2] The Houdinis of tennis are the teaching professionals. Average players flock to them in the hope that magic can be performed. Then there's the next level, where lessons are augmented by books promising fantastic results.

the risk of humiliation—when you can sit back in the calm and security of the clubhouse?

6. Nothing ventured, nothing gained.

SYMPTOM: The player seldom varies from a stereotype of play, preferring instead to fall into patterns of shots that make it easy to anticipate his moves.

ANALYSIS: More ritual. One of the elements involved in playing good tennis is that of surprise, but many players rely on prescribed forms of play that offer all the unpredictability of shopping for groceries. Early in his life a person begins to repeat certain behavioral patterns in the form of games, and these eventually lead to personal coherence and a sense of style. Today, the memories of these ritualistic games are fond, familiar, and safe. As a result, the player feels comfortable maintaining a safe and predictable type of tennis game which runs the risk of solidifying into an unvarying pattern. (In other words, another security blanket.) It's not that he doesn't realize that taking risks is part of the game; it's just that he feels much more secure within the confines of repetition. When this player is teamed with a partner who can't hit anywhere but directly at his opponent, ritual covers the court like smog.

7. Everything ventured, nothing gained.

SYMPTOM: The player relies consistently on unpredictable but low-percentage shots (often trying to clobber the ball at inopportune times), preferring their overuse to a steady method which would undoubtedly be more profitable.

ANALYSIS: This impatient character is the counterpart of the previous one, which would be all right if he didn't push his style to the opposite extreme. In many cases he's an impatient person with a built-in defiance of limits (which probably started when he constantly went against his parents' wishes), and he's not going to do particularly well in a restrictive game like tennis. The propriety and rigidity of the game are simply more than he can bear, and he impulsively strikes out at its boundaries with erratic results.

In addition, the risk taker has some of the principal characteristics of the Las Vegas gambler: he's out to "make a killing." Usually, though, the gambler fears retaliation for such impulses. If he should somehow get what he's after—which doesn't happen frequently—he then anxiously turns around and blames the "killing" on lady luck and sets out to lose his easily gotten gains. "I didn't win myself," he assures himself, "therefore I'm not responsible. Easy come, easy go." The risk taker may be a person who hopes he'll win but doesn't want any part of victory's implications.

8. Here today, gone tomorrow. Or is it gone today, here tomorrow?

SYMPTOM: The player shows absolutely no consistency in his game, playing a marvelous set one day and a horrendous one the next.

ANALYSIS: Dr. Jekyll and Mr. Hyde is alive and well and living on the tennis court. Perhaps no single problem plagues the average player to the degree of this dreaded inconsistency. Like a fever, it can have several diagnoses. But first the player should *expect* intermittent outside interference with his game. The short circuits of life can jam a backhand and cause tennis tensions more quickly than anything known to modern man. But those for whom the only certain thing in tennis is uncertainty itself are probably experiencing a more specific problem with sustaining aggression. They flop back and forth between asserting themselves and not asserting themselves (in life as well as on the court, most likely). As their guilt over aggression rises and falls, so does the quality of their tennis.

9. "Everything was beautiful. Then we started to play."

SYMPTOM: The player has an excellent "warm-up," hitting the ball firmly and precisely, but when the game begins he can't hit a lick.

ANALYSIS: This is an ailment as common to tennis as the double fault. Although the game is one of the safest arenas imaginable, many players still have inhibitions about competing there. When winning and losing aren't on the line these players can look like lions; when play starts they're more like lambs. Why? Probably they're not comfortable with their own aggression when they know the game is for real. Being aggressive and wanting to win so badly goes against their self-images as proper people who wouldn't harm the proverbial fly. Good gracious, competition means *winning*, and the urge to win upsets them. For many of these people the claim that "it's not whether you win or lose" has been tattooed on their psyches.

10. The Infinite Rallier

SYMPTOM: The player never tries actually to win points outright, preferring instead to make sure the ball stays in play.

ANALYSIS: This is something of a variation of the last two types. The idea of actually trying to win a point—except through an opponent's error—is completely foreign to the Infinite Rallier. Such attempts to win might constitute a display of aggression, which makes this type uneasy. He feels much better standing at the baseline, where no harm can be done. If there's anything that makes the Infinite Rallier more nervous than winning a point, it's rushing the net *and* winning a point. He can be counted on to avoid both as if they are pestilence and famine. "You hit a few, I'll hit a few," he thinks. "Back and forth we go. Oops, I hit one out of your reach. Sorry about that. I'll try not to let it happen again." A few members of this clan have confided the intense satisfaction of having won a match purely on their opponent's mistakes.

11. The Perpetual Lesson Taker

SYMPTOM: The player will spend hours on end with the nearest tennis pro, but when invited to play a game he will always have a reason prepared to avoid such a confrontation.

ANALYSIS: If they're cagey, this is how people who think like types eight and nine can avoid competition and aggression in the first place. Instead of facing such matters of substance, the Perpetual Lesson Taker is forever able to concentrate on form and shape. The excuses such a critter can invent to avoid a real match are fairly standard. They range all the way from "My backhand needs more work" to "My *pro* thinks my backhand needs more work." If the instructor should turn up sick one day, this player can always fall back on the ball machine. By forever whacking meaningless shots, he or she can maintain a clear conscience. Like the Social Climber, the Perpetual Lesson Taker may be a terrific tennis player, but no one will ever know for sure, least of all himself.

12. I don't want it, you can have it.

SYMPTOM: As soon as the player wins an ad point, he invariably manages to lose the next point and get the score back to deuce.

ANALYSIS: More often than not, this is a person of the variety for whom the prospect of victory is less than scintillating. As with the three previous types, the idea of winning through aggression does not rest easily on his shoulders. He feels very good when things are even (it has been claimed in several quarters that this player is responsible for the expression "Go to the deuce") but lives in mortal fear of beating his opponent by a large margin. Somewhere in his tennis bag is a large amount of guilt. When particularly under the influence of this concoction he has been known to follow his own infrequently well-played shots with one word: "Sorry."

13. The Fast-Fading Failure

SYMPTOM: The player repeatedly loses sets in which he was once comfortably ahead.

ANALYSIS: Almost a twin of the last familiar face, this person is saying, "I don't want it, you can have it" on a somewhat grander scale. "I'm a good sport," he adds. "A regular nonaggressor, that's me." But there may be something else at work here. There is a certain type of person who starts things in life but can never finish them. We find him always beginning vast numbers of projects and not seeing them through. His car has one newly waxed fender and his lawn always seems half-mowed. He is incapable of sustaining energy and excitement. There are usually many complex reasons for this, but among them is probably the need to disappoint himself and others. On the tennis court he has decided that winning would mean the satisfactory completion of something he started, and he subconsciously avoids it at all costs, even if it means blowing a 5–0 lead.

14. The Loser

SYMPTOM: The player has difficulty winning at tennis, even if his opponents usually are not as good as he is.

ANALYSIS: Unlike the Fast-Fading Failure, this person often doesn't even get to enjoy building a big lead. He simply goes out on the court and loses from the beginning, often to people who know in their hearts that they have no business beating him. Chances are our Loser in tennis may be a "loser in life" as well. He's inclined to embrace defeat of all sorts, and there may be multiple reasons for this: love of suffering, the need to capitulate to certain people in order to gain love, fears of overinflation of self-esteem, and so on. But more than likely the main problem is one we've seen again and again: fear of one's aggression and what it will do to someone else. "Don't take me too seriously," the Loser almost seems to be saying. "I'm not going to beat you or hurt you. If I get to the point where I think I could hurt you, I'll stop." Which he subconsciously does, right at the start.

15. The Reluctant Smasher

SYMPTOM: The player is normally considered a "big hitter" but can't seem to get any velocity on the ball when playing a "soft hitter."

ANALYSIS: The Reluctant Smasher, normally a slugger of immensely powerful shots, often appears to be overcome by paralysis when confronted by a weaker player. Somehow, slow and arching shots from across the net deaden his racquet. "It's all a matter of rebound" is the type of conclusion he makes. "If my opponent doesn't hit the ball hard, it won't rebound well off my racquet." O.K., but the problem is probably more mental than physical. The smasher—powerful ox that he is—may be subconsciously guilt-ridden at the idea of unleashing aggression in the direction of what appears to be a mild-mannered opponent, or toward someone whom he identifies as a "victim." The tennis battlefield is littered with the corpses of such smashers who were soundly defeated and whose last words were "But I can hit the ball so much *harder* than he can." Yes, but they often don't, allowing the pace of their games to wind down to the point where they poke along with their opponents' games. At which time the opponents, who are much more familiar with a slow game, can be seen smacking their lips.

16. The Patty-caker

SYMPTOM: The player, although apparently physically able, does not hit the ball hard.

ANALYSIS: This person appears to be a mystery: broad shoulders and large arms deliver sitting ducks which set up his pie-eyed opponents for the kill. Yet the courts are filled with people who—despite the fact tennis is a socially acceptable outlet which permits them to vent pent-up pushiness—simply can't mobilize aggressiveness. The motives for this may be as varied as the people afflicted, but the result is a flock of Patty-cakers all flailing at the ball and sending it nowhere. True, sometimes the reasons are muscular. More often, they are firmly grounded in conflicts with aggression. For women (see Chapter 7) the problem may be particularly acute.

17. "Listen, I'm sorry about that shot, but I think the other team is coming to the net now so maybe we should change our strategy, and do you like my new tennis shorts which I bought the other day at the same place I bought my racquet the week before, and speaking of racquets . . ."

SYMPTOM: The player talks on the court seemingly all the time.

ANALYSIS: When some people are ill at ease or angry over a particularly bad shot, they may curse aloud and may even reach the point of tossing a racquet or ball. But many players, aware that such behavior is frowned upon in this game of great sanctity, choose to find other ways of discharging feelings about ineptness, aggression, and anxiety. More than a few of them have hit upon constant chatter as a way. Not only does this answer the urge to do *something* when the game goes awry, it also provides a way to prove that the talker is really a swell person who wouldn't dream of doing anything outrageous on the court. "See," the talker is saying (inside his head this time, rather than out of his mouth), "I'm really a cordial sort of guy. The fact that I just hit a shot off the ceiling doesn't bother me at all." Meanwhile, you know damn well it's killing him.

18. The Continual Apologizer

SYMPTOM: "I'm sorry . . . I'm sorry . . . I'm sorry . . . I'm sorry."

ANALYSIS: As we stated in Chapter 2, the Continual Apologizer is most likely talking to himself rather than to his opponents or partners. There seem to be two times when this happens: when a player is doing badly and when a player is doing well. In short, "sorry" knows no bounds. The person who is constantly apologizing when he isn't playing well is probably failing to live up to his image of his ideal self. He's disappointed in himself and feels the need to apologize (again to himself) for his own play. The player who apologizes while he wins (and there are more of these people around that you may think) is probably imagining himself to be hurting and/or humiliating his opponent. Even if he doesn't think he's being malicious, he may feel awkward placing someone in a losing position. In either case, "sorry" maintains its place as the tennis player's favorite on-court word.

19. The Continual Berater

SYMPTOM: "Oh, I'm a fool . . . a bungler . . . an idiot . . . an oaf . . . a jerk. . . ."

ANALYSIS: All hail the King of the Inner Dialogue. The Continual Berater is the flip side of the Continual Apologizer. "I'm sorry" has been replaced by a string of insults aimed at the self, but the motive remains the same: failure to match the image flickering on the internal television screen. Sometimes it seems as if the Continual Berater expects insults to arrive in the form of defeat and bad play but has chosen to beat them to the punch. "I'll criticize myself before they can do it to me," he seems to be saying to himself. "That way it won't hurt so much."

20. What's the score?

SYMPTOM: The player habitually forgets the score.

ANALYSIS: Admittedly, whoever invented the traditional scoring system for tennis must have been something of a sadist. Either that, or he believed the terms "one," "two," and "three" to be obsolete. In any case, there does seem to be an inordinately large number of people playing the game who show a striking ability to forget what happened to them only fifteen seconds before. This could indicate particularly good concentration on the game, but we've noticed that it tends to happen more to players when they're anxious about losing.

Players who repeatedly lose track of the score are probably related to Perpetual Lesson Takers and Infinite Ralliers.

Forgetting who's winning helps eliminate the notion of competition, which in turn means there's no real aggression taking place. "How can this be 'for keeps,' " the forgetful player is subconsciously asking himself, "if there's no score?"

21. Life and death on the tennis court.

SYMPTOM: The player takes the game as seriously as if he were performing on the center court at Wimbledon.

ANALYSIS: How well we all recognize this type's grim visage as he marches from baseline to net and back again. He won't crack a smile from the warm-up to the shower. Even his own decent shots don't bring a kind word from his tightly pursed lips. People like this are often quite successful and seek perfection in tennis as well as in life. (Not necessarily to knock it, but "doing well" is a necessity for obsessive/compulsive persons.) For some of these folks, the game becomes a measure of human worth, so that playing it badly—even for an hour—can turn them into total failures. Tennis is about as much a game for these people as is going swimming with sharks. If they don't turn the game into a matter of living or dying, they feel it's not really worth their time. "If I'm doing this," their inner dialogues ask, "it must be important, right?" "Right," they answer themselves. "And so are you."

22. Laugh and dance on the tennis court.

SYMPTOM: The player takes the game as seriously as if he were playing on center stage at the Palladium as a stand-up comedian.

ANALYSIS: A laugh a minute, this particular player. He hits out and giggles, hits the net cord and guffaws. A so-called good sport? Perhaps not. Like many of the other characters we've examined in this chapter, he may be serious about not being taken seriously. In order to deny his aggressive and rivalrous feelings, he cavorts around the court pretending to be a clown in whites. "It's only a game," he titters, leaning over backward to convince his fellow players that nothing really matters. But, of course, it matters a great deal to *him* as he dances along the white lines, laughing on the outside and crying on the inside.

23. The Doomsayer

SYMPTOM: The player displays an uncanny ability to predict accurately just when his game will fall apart.

ANALYSIS: "I know I can't keep playing this well," the Doomsayer says to his opponent. Before long he's right. This phenomenon is no accident, of course. Even players to whom it happens all the time will declare, "I *made* it happen by worrying about it." Which is true in a way, although the player seldom realizes why. For one thing, too great a rise in self-esteem can lead to defensive self-fulfilling prophecies. "I'm really not this good; therefore, this lob will be lousy." For another, he may associate victory with being unpopular. "If I win, I'm not going to be accepted." Predicting failure—and having the prediction come true—is his way of saying, "Don't worry about me, and for God's sake don't take me seriously."

24. The Living, Breathing Bundle of Hurt

SYMPTOM: The player whose calls are questioned becomes upset to the point that his game is adversely affected.

ANALYSIS: Until some sort of magic electronic system is invented as a substitute, amateur tennis players will have to continue to be their own referees—or, more accurately, referees for their opponents. This can lead to all kinds of tricky problems (see Chapter 6), particularly in this game which attracts people by its aura of honesty and halo of propriety. Most tennis players consider themselves bastions of morality, and any question of their honesty in calling shots is an affront to the ideal self. From there it's a mere drop shot to interference with concentration and loss of control.

25. The Living, Breathing Bundle of Excuses

SYMPTOM: The player blames his bad play and defeat on all things imaginable, with the exception of himself.

ANALYSIS: The strings. The grip. The weight. The balance. And these excuses involve only the *racquet,* so you can guess how many more reasons for losing this person has in his tennis bag of tricks. The existence of such excuses shouldn't be surprising, because so many of us use them. The reason is a fundamental one: the difference between the actual self and the ideal self again. Poor play widens the distance between the two, a state of affairs that causes the player increasing anxiety and embarrassment. To prevent further separation he clamps on the brakes by proclaiming that what is happening really isn't happening at all. *He's* not really playing badly, you see; it's the fault of the court, or the net, or the lights, or the balls, or the background, or any of a hundred other things. The distance between the two selves is thereby lessened—at least in his imagination.

26. The Rotten Apple

SYMPTOM: The player worries, particularly in doubles, that his poor play is spoiling the game for others on the court.

ANALYSIS: The Rotten Apple contains certain traits of both the Continual Apologizer and the Doomsayer. "I'm sorry for what's about to happen," he often says, even before he begins to play badly. Like the Apologizer, he probably isn't taking aim at someone else. He's not really worried about hurting the game for other people; he's worried about ruining it for *himself.* He's unhappy about being the worst player on the court. When he fails to live up to his ideal self-image, he transfers the disappointment to his opponents and partners. "Boy, are *they* having a lousy time," he decides, and this helps minimize the gap between the two selves. In the meantime he's using the Doomsayer's ploy of getting accepted as a nice guy because he really isn't a threat or a winner.

27. The Overanalyzer

SYMPTOM: The player ends his matches by dissecting everything he thinks he did wrong.

ANALYSIS: Like the Equipment Freak, the Overanalyzer is fascinated by the idea of magic. He subconsciously believes that if he talks about his problems enough, they'll disappear in some mysterious fashion. People who constantly discuss their illnesses are often attempting the same ploy.

In addition, the Overanalyzer is particularly good at not quite remembering the way events *really* took place. That poor approach shot at a particularly crucial juncture, he may conclude, came awfully close. Well, didn't it? In truth, no. What the Overanalyzer is really hoping is that the moment occurred the way he wanted it to occur. He wishes it had matched his dreams, when in reality it wasn't very close. Once again we find a player who is desperately trying to bridge the widening river between what he thinks is happening and what is really happening.

28. The Ogler/Voyeur

SYMPTOM: The player cannot keep from constantly glancing at players on adjoining courts, sometimes even delaying his own game during such opportunities.

ANALYSIS: If a group of tennis courts can be likened to a community, the Oglers are the nosy neighbors who are out to keep up with the Joneses. Their insistence on checking out what's happening on the court next door indicates low self-esteem. In fact, ogling tends to increase in an inverse ratio to the Ogler's own quality of play: fewer good shots mean more watching. Later, persistent ogling can lead straight to Voyeurism. As explained in Chapter 4, the Voyeur is involved in much more than honest admiration. What's taking place here is stone cold envy. Voyeurs want to take into themselves what they see, and in this case they're after a catlike net game or a crunching service. Such longings not only hint at faulty self-esteem but also can further lower one's emotional poise. The vicious circle marches 'round and 'round the courts.

29. The Prima Donna

SYMPTOM: The player feels he must be the center of attention on the court and isn't afraid to tell you the reasons why.

ANALYSIS: If you don't believe the Prima Donna is a superb player, just ask him. Actually, such vanity in reasonable doses will probably help your game, since it involves pride in your accomplishments. But for the Prima Donna the need for internal pride has grown into an excessive quest for external approval. His eye is no longer on the ball (indeed, he often bungles his many intended smashes) but is focused clearly on the show he is putting on for an audience that is either real or imagined. Some players wilt at the sight of spectators, but for the Prima Donna they are the rays of sunshine that cover the court during his search for perfection and complete mastery. Because he hasn't internalized a good sense of self-approval, he seeks it outside himself through the roar of the crowd—even though, in this case, the roar of the crowd probably consists of little more than an occasional "good shot" from opponents and partners.

30. The Tennis Parent (A Legend in Its Own Time)

SYMPTOM: The parent relentlessly pushes his or her son or daughter into competitive tennis.

ANALYSIS: "Behind every tennis player there is another tennis player" is the way the saying goes, and in a remarkable number of cases the pusher is either Mom or Dad. Many top competitive tennis players are driven by a strong wish for parental approval—frequently the son for mother's and the daughter for father's. From the parents' point of view, this means a chance to live vicariously through their kids. If you've never achieved your ideal, what better way to take up the chase than through your son or daughter? It's a perfect set-up: at just about the time a tennis-playing parent reaches middle age and realizes his or her dreams of glory are unrealizable, along come the children to provide a sense of continuity. In this way—as the parent slowly tries to deal with anxieties about dying—he or she is comforted by the knowledge that the quest for the perfect backhand—and immortality—lives on.

31. The Uninvited Player-Coach

SYMPTOM: The player offers advice to partners, opponents, and anyone else who will stop long enough to listen, even though they don't remember hearing themselves ask for any help.

ANALYSIS: Perhaps no one is greeted on the tennis court with quite as much disdain as this persistent interloper. (He should be distinguished, however, from the more welcomed adviser whose remarks are infrequent and well chosen.) Nothing seems to jab at self-esteem more than repeated unsolicited suggestions for improvement. Recipients of such unwanted advice should know that the Uninvited Player-Coach is probably resentful that he has been paired with what appears to be a poor player. But don't take it personally. In all probability, he's the type to find fault in people everywhere, not just on the tennis court. He's like a presumptuous oldest child lording over his siblings. "See," he may be saying to himself, "this is how *I* do it. Perfectly." This, of course, is often what most angers the "pupil," particularly if he knows that the "coach" is only a rung or two above him in ability.

32. The Commander-in-Chief

SYMPTOM: The player, in doubles, enjoys telling his partner what to do and spends a great deal of time inventing strategy to cope with his opponents.

ANALYSIS: Like the Uninvited Player-Coach, the Commander-in-Chief seems to be very adept at making enemies on the tennis court. "Don't hit to Al! . . . Move up! . . . Down the alley! . . . Let it go! . . . Crosscourt! . . . Back up!" Ever the typical obsessive/compulsive, the Commander needs to control situations but resents being controlled himself. (Obviously, he has a power struggle ahead if his partner turns out to have similar obsessive/compulsive tendencies.) As is the case with the Uninvited Player-Coach, the Commander is giving his threatened ego a shot in the arm. If his orders lead to victory, he'll be the first to say he told you so. In defeat, however, he's not likely to say very much about who was in charge.

33. The Rabid Congratulator

SYMPTOM: The player heaps excessive praise and congratulations upon his opponents and partners.

ANALYSIS: Like the Continual Apologizer, the Rabid Congratulator is talking to himself more than to anyone else. Those constant calls across the net are likely to be aimed at his own self-esteem rather than at his opponent's, since he is likely to be suffering from a sense of inferiority. He is trying to pull up his faltering ego by its bootstraps, and failure to do so will leave him prone to depressive slumps. "Congratulations, you played well," he says aloud to his opponent after he loses. He is fishing for the beginning of that never-ending string of compliments which flows among tennis players, hoping to hear something like "Thanks, but you played well yourself." One way to find out if your opponent is sincere about his congratulations is to answer with something along the lines of "Yeah, I really *did* play well, didn't I?" If you're in the company of a Rabid Congratulator, expect to hear no more.

34. "I always play better against someone who's better than I am." (An Official Tennis Rule of Law)

SYMPTOM: The player feels his game improves in direct proportion to the abilities of his opponents.

ANALYSIS: How true, how true. Good players seem to bring out the best in us, bad players the worst. All of us tend to feel this way, and it's probably not our imaginations. Being in the company of good players (whom we often define as those who are better than we are) does wonders for our egos. Conversely, playing with bad players (or those who are worse than we are) lowers self-esteem. Unless we're in a game that is totally over our heads, a good opponent or partner makes us feel that we're worth something. "Wow, if he's on the court with me I must be pretty good." This is one of the clearest examples you'll ever find of increased self-esteem improving your game.

There's also the matter of freeing guilt. People feel easier about being aggressive toward someone who's strong and "can take it." Like a child slamming a fist into Daddy's enormous open palm, a relatively weak player is comforted by the knowledge that his stronger opponent won't crumble or necessarily retaliate. Love prevails—at least for now—on the tennis court.

6

Some Cheat, Some Choke

Case study: RHODA, age 40

For Rhoda tennis became important relatively late in life. She had grown up in the city, the second of three daughters born to the head of a small custodial services company and his pleasant, inoffensive wife. She felt a great attachment to her father, a weekend tennis player who used to take the family on some sort of an outing almost every week when the weather was good. On these occasions they sometimes took long walks together during which he would assure her that she was his favorite daughter. (He often verbalized fantasies in which the two of them ran away together.) She reacted by behaving in a very girlish and charming way, but she also noticed with some alarm that her father would later be very solicitous of her mother and two sisters. During high school she puzzled over the increasing distance between the two of them. When he died suddenly during Rhoda's second year in college, she sensed that something had never quite been completed in their relationship.

She married shortly after graduation, choosing a man whom she could manipulate as easily as she thought she had controlled her father. The courtship was brief, the marriage more elopement than ceremony. The childless union worked well for a while, but Rhoda's husband eventually grew more and more distant, finally enveloping himself in his myriad business ventures while disdaining the coquettishness he had once found so fascinating in his wife. The ensuing divorce was painful for Rhoda, and after its conclusion she moved to another part of the country, near her older sister.

She took up tennis about six years ago, mostly for something to do. The divorce settlement had been a good one, and she was working only part-time as a secretary, though her major in college had been economics. Within eighteen months of taking up the game she belonged to two clubs. She can now be found on the courts two or three times a week and has reached the point where she plays—and occasionally even wins—"B"-level tournaments. However, Rhoda is aware that she has a bad habit on the court, one that has nothing to do with shot making.

She cheats.

Not all the time, mind you. And not enough that anyone seems to notice. But enough to bother her, at least after the fact. She is quite aware that in the long run it is part of a self-defeating pattern. Yet no matter how much she tells herself, "You know better than that," she finds herself nibbling away here and there, making "out" calls when she's not completely sure that the ball wasn't indeed "in." "It only happens when the chips are down," she rationalizes, but then worries that "I just don't seem to be able to resist the temptation."

In the course of undergoing therapy Rhoda has been able to become a more "honest" player and limit some of her self-defeating actions. It is clear that she was cheating at tennis as a way of letting out anger and resentment while expressing her hypertrophic sense of entitlement. She felt life had cheated her because her mother had been "nothing" in her life and had been absorbed in caring for her younger sister. Her sense of injury found expression in a tendency to break the rules. Her self-esteem had been deeply injured by all these people, particularly by the discovery of her father's solicitous behavior toward the other women in his life. She had long ago learned how to manipulate situations by being coy and cute. Making inaccurate calls was simply another way of doing this. In coming to realize the hidden motives for her cheating, Rhoda has all but eliminated the tendency—although she still admits to moments when she feels she has acted less than honorably.

What's this? Cheating in tennis? Oh no, surely not in tennis, where the Grantland Rice homily—"It's not whether you win or lose but how you play the game"—is supposedly engraved upon the solid-gold heart of every player. Cheating is heard as a discouraging word on these courts of justice, an intruder from darker games which would best be banished along with everyone who hasn't paid this year's club membership dues. At best, cheating at tennis is rather bemusedly referred to as "gamesmanship" and is generally treated in the game's less serious literature with a good guffaw. Its practitioners are described as the types who would sic Doberman pinschers on their opponents or wash down the opposite end of the court with diesel oil. That sort of thing. [1]

But what about the allegedly true story of the player who was waiting to return service while holding match point during the finals of a local tournament? Wasting no time, he drove the first serve down the line for a clean winner and happily leaped the net to shake hands with his opponent. The server, however, was still waiting at the baseline, calmly bouncing the other ball. "Sorry, old chum," he announced with a wry smile, "but I'm calling a foot fault on myself on that one. Second service."

To the server that might be gamesmanship. The receiver has another word for it: cheating.

It's time to face the truth. Although it has never been statistically proven, we suspect tennis players probably trail only golfers and politicians as the world's most prolific cheaters. This is not, however, to say that most of them are willful and cold-blooded swindlers (though we are not prepared to make the same modification for golfers and politicians). Some players probably don't even realize they're cheating on the tennis court. And for an even larger number, the motives for making inaccurate calls are so entrenched in their psyches that their actions could hardly be termed cold-blooded. In fact, cheating at tennis—which we'll define here as simply *trying to win through deception*—often involves deception of the *self*

---

[1] This is not to suggest that the notorious "psyche-out" does not exist in tennis. Shelves of light and entertaining books have been written on this subject, but with little serious advice on how to cope with it. See Chapter 9.

as well as of opponents. In the same way they discover tennis to be a safe way to bind aggression, many players seem to find the court a convenient place to break rules without provoking severe retaliation.

Ironically, this game in which whiteness is both literal and figurative also provides more opportunities to cheat than almost any other sport. Included in the very civility of the game is the notion that its players shall police themselves, that is, make their own decisions, particularly line calls. Unless you do a lot of your playing at Longwood in August or Forest Hills in September, you must act as your own referee, umpire, and linesperson. What's more, you don't determine the accuracy of your *own* shots, but instead make judgments on your opponents' play. This is strange indeed, not unlike the concept of a baseball batter being declared responsible for deciding whether the pitcher is throwing strikes or balls. Further, the sheer number of calls that must be made in a game of tennis is astounding.[2] Even allowing for the number of shots that are not the least bit questionable, a player can expect dozens of opportunities to cheat every time he plays. So why should it be so surprising when he does?

But surprising it is. Targets of cheaters often react as if they have just witnessed an armed robbery of the local parish house. "Good God, man, is nothing sacred?" Part of the draw of tennis, after all, is truth, justice, and the American way. At first, the cheated may actually be only mildly annoyed by what has happened. "Are you *sure* that was out?" he will ask, barely shifting his tone of voice into the interrogative. After that he can really only drop the matter, knowing full well that he shouldn't make a scene on the court. If the cheating should

[2] And probably indeterminable. In one particular 1976 match between professionals Bjorn Borg and Guillermo Vilas, *one point* lasted eighty-five shots. Jack Nicklaus doesn't hit the ball that many times in an entire round of golf, a game that is purported to provide numerous opportunities for cheating.

be particularly obvious or continual, however, the victim's irritation may turn to anger.

This can lead to surprising results, as was the case with Tony, a fifty-year-old junior high school principal. Having played tennis since his teens, Tony imagined that he had seen almost everything on the tennis court. Until he met one particular opponent, that is.

"I was attending a convention during the summer, and a few of us had brought along our tennis racquets. On the second morning I managed to grab one of the hotel's courts at the suggestion of another principal I'd met the night before who said he'd like to play me. I don't usually play singles anymore, but he was roughly my vintage so I figured he wouldn't run my legs off. Just a friendly game, I thought. Brother, was I wrong. This guy was the damnedest, most bold-faced cheater I'd ever seen in my life. At first I thought he was kidding with some of his calls, and when I realized he wasn't, I was incensed. I got so mad that I decided to run him into the ground. I don't remember when I've ever hit the ball that well from corner to corner. Certainly not in the last few years. I don't think I missed a single putaway. I didn't care how old he was—and it turned out he was older than I am—I was going to make the sonofabitch run. I beat him 6–3, 6–0. I felt a little bad about it later, but I sure didn't feel sorry out there on the court."

What happened to Tony is obvious. The repeated incidents of cheating legitimized the aggression that normally would have been inhibited by his opponent's age. Freed from guilt, he was able to play a devastating, even destructive game. Reactions to cheating vary. Some people become intimidated by the sense of injustice it creates. Most cheaters, though, should be prepared for the surges of wrath, sense of injury, and subsequent aggression they may incur in opponents.

(If there are Theories of Relativity pertaining to the cheater and the cheated in tennis, they appear to be as follows: 1. If the cheater is a worse player than the cheated, the latter is probably going to be spurred on to more damaging heights; conversely, if the cheater is a better player, the cheated is likely to feel even more helpless. 2. The more a person plays opponents who are over his or her head, the more he or she is likely to cheat. Equality induces respect, while superiority stimulates magnanimity. 3. The further a person falls behind during a game, the more likely he or she is to cheat.)

But the urge to cheat at games does not appear for the first time when one walks out of the sporting goods store with the first tennis racquet and can of balls. The impulse seems to be a universal experience for children. Most repress it because of training, ideals, or guilt, but its lingering presence heightens their awareness that others are probably ready if not willing to cheat *them*. (The well-known Oedipus complex—the attachment of the child to the parent of the opposite sex, accompanied by aggressive and envious feelings toward the parent of the same sex—may become a prototype for cheating in its attempt to break the rules. Rhoda, described at the beginning of this chapter, is a case in point. She felt cheated out of her birthright and therefore entitled to cheat at tennis.) Those children who want to win so badly may be revealing a fragile sense of self-esteem as well as a limited ability to empathize with others. The fact that they do cheat probably indicates a magical desire for mastery and perfection not dissimilar to the wish that will turn up years later on the tennis court: that an opponent's crosscourt shot will be out, thereby preserving victory. To ensure that the shot is considered out, the player need only say so—whether the call is accurate or not.

As we have suggested, the number of conscious tennis cheaters—the type who say to themselves, "I'm cheating and I don't give a damn about it"—appears to be very small. At the other end of the scale, making up a somewhat larger group, are the completely unconscious cheaters. Ironically, they "honestly" don't believe they're cheating. They're the

people who are deceiving themselves as well as their opponents. The last and perhaps largest group of cheaters play
somewhere between these two poles. These players aren't
ruthless in their deception, but just can't seem to resist temptation. If any sort of ambiguity arises—say, if an opponent
wonders aloud, "Was that in?" after one of his shots nicks the
line—they are the people who will invariably decide in their
own favor regardless of the fact the hallowed "Code" of the
United States Tennis Association specifically proclaims that
"any doubt must be resolved in favor of his opponent." [3] Or
maybe this type of player won't be in a particular hurry to
"call against himself any ball that he clearly sees out on his opponent's side of the net," which the Code also advises. Theirs
is more a reluctant nibble at the game's mores than a full bite,
more passive than active cheating. But cheating nonetheless.

When is cheating most likely to occur on the court? Based
on our observations, it centers around the following, which
are listed in order of decreasing frequency.

The Serve

Receiving service puts a player in his or her moment of
great vulnerability. Often the ball zips past before a reaction
can be considered, never mind made. This combination of
helplessness and/or humiliation can lead to the quest for a
magical solution. Ergo: "Out!"

The Baseline

Common sense tells players that they are less likely to
provoke conflict if they cheat on shots that land as far away
from their opponents as possible. ("A player who stands at
one baseline and questions a ball that lands near the other

[3] Colonel Nick Powel, *The Code* (Princeton, N.J.: United States Tennis Association, 1974). This is a fascinating little booklet, a tract on morality that only tennis
could have come up with, and the contents of which many of its players don't have
the slightest knowledge about. It is of no little interest that the booklet makes repeated and specific references to "cheating" in tennis.

baseline is most likely being ridiculous," admits the Code.) Besides, when Major Walter Clopton Wingfield founded modern lawn tennis in 1873, he made cheating in the back-court easier by placing the net at such a height that it oc-casionally cuts the line of sight that runs between a player and the opposite baseline.

The Sideline

This offers the most infrequent possibilities to get away with less-than-honest line calls. According to the laws of paral-lax, opponents can sight *down* a line more easily than *across*.

The Score

A point or two is sometimes picked up by forgetting the score or taking advantage of the fact that your opponent does not remember it. The first situation, unless forgetting is habitual, may be an unconscious attempt to gain a little some-thing extra. "If I forget, maybe *he'll* forget," the thinking goes, "and who knows how much I'll gain?" Using an oppo-nent's poor memory, which is a more conscious ploy, simply involves replying "Right!" when asked before serving if the score is, say, deuce. But only if it's really 15–40.

Miscellaneous

There are infrequent moments when a technicality is called upon to salvage a point: the receiver claiming a serve just touched the net after it had already zipped past; a player denying a "double bounce"; swearing you thought your oppo-nent's racquet flicked the net; the receiver arguing that he wasn't "quite ready" when his opponent served an ace; or a player noting that it certainly looked as if the person on the other end of the court just made a "double hit." And, of course, one can always claim a foot fault here and there, though such allegations are usually received in nontour-

nament matches with enough incredulity to render them
worthless.

In addition to the more prevalent run-of-the-mill "just-an-
inch-out" cheaters, the tennis courts have a marvelous ability
to turn up other, more specialized varieties. There are the
gallant cheaters, for instance. They want to "take two" shots
at the slightest provocation, which may range from the reflection off an opponent's bald pate to the yelp of a dog three
courts over. The gallant cheater is always grasping at the
slightest straws. "Oh, you think it's 4–2? Coulda sworn it was
4–3. Let's see now, I won the last game, or was it you? And
the game before that I hit a backhand crosscourt . . ." and so
on, ad infinitum.

Then there are the *reverse cheaters*, for whom what's "out"
must be called "in." Besides being seen as a tremendous in-
sult by opponents, the actions of such players may indicate
hunger for approval. They play tennis less to win games than
to win friends. They feel threatened by any potential loss of
love and strive to avoid this by coming across as humble ser-
vants bearing gifts. Meanwhile, some of their opponents are
less than grateful. Others may be seething.

And let's not overlook the *uncertain cheaters*, for whom
"Play It Again" is a life motto. They are unsure of their calls,
consistently requesting that points be replayed (even though
the venerable Code dictates that a ball that can't be called out
with certainty is good). In fact, this may go deeper than cheating at tennis. Obsessive/compulsive personalities are often
such wishy-washy players who can't decide "in" or "out." [4]
Off the court, they frequently have a deep inability to make
decisions. Meanwhile, their on-court actions with regard to
calls are a kind of pseudocheating designed to keep them in
this state of uncertainty.

Motives for cheating depend on the player and the type of

---

[4] After age forty, however, one's visual and other reflexes decline, leading to
greater difficulty in calling questionable shots.

deception being carried out. To each his own, as it were. The *willful cheater*, for example, may be rationalizing his actions by telling himself he's decided to break the rules in order to beat opponents to the punch. He's like the kid who's decided he knows what all the other kids are up to: "Sure, everyone cheats at tennis. So why shouldn't I?" Closely akin to this type—though perhaps not always as deliberate—is the *touchy personality*. He or she is overly suspicious of life in general and is quick to imagine all sorts of evil motives in others. As a result, cheating becomes an attempt to redress such conjecture, but without any of the glib openness of the intentional rule bender.

Other cheaters who are not wholly conscious of what they are doing may have decided that life itself is a cheat which they are out to rectify. Rhoda, found at the beginning of this chapter, is a good example. Others may feel they are not particularly attractive. Still others might actually have suffered a series of severe financial setbacks. In any case, cheating (and one of its purposes, which is winning) is a way to bolster low self-images. Unscrupulousness—though perhaps unintentional—becomes a method of overcoming feelings of inadequacy.

For there are certain people for whom life cannot exist unless it involves a certain amount of risk. To them the aggression found in tennis is of little interest. They're after *excitement* on the court. Maybe they're characters out of Chapter 5 (number seven) who'll attempt a lot of high-risk shots. Or maybe they'll titillate themselves by unconsciously trying to get away with a bit of rule breaking. To these people the very act of cheating is more thrilling than the points to be gained by it, the smashing of boundaries more satisfying than winning. Others gratify their need to feel unjustly treated in life by cheating, inviting accusation, and then feeling thoroughly justified in launching self-righteous counterattacks which provide more pleasure than a well-placed crosscourt.

But if there is a single major motive for cheating on the tennis court, it is one that the Code has picked up on: "Some players will insist that on occasion even though a ball is good they want it to be out so badly that they will unconsciously call it out. This reasoning is difficult for a strong-willed fair-minded player to accept." We're not so sure that most players are aware enough of why they're cheating—or even that they *are* cheating—to recognize that this is the reason, let alone "insist" upon it. But it does seem to us that *wanting* the ball to be out is the principal motive for most of the deception that takes place on the tennis court.

One way to examine this is to hear two rather different sides of the same story. The first side comes from Del, a forty-four-year-old accountant who found himself playing a tournament match against Ron, one of his frequent informal opponents.

"Ron and I had played, oh gosh, maybe fifty times. It got so we knew each other's style a little too well, actually. That's why I was a bit disappointed when we drew each other in the opening round of the club tournament. It was the first tournament for both of us, and we were hoping to get to play some other people. I was particularly irked because Ron beats me three times out of four, so this meant I probably wouldn't get to the second round. But when we started playing, I found myself doing well. Or maybe I found Ron doing badly. I won the first set—it was a best-two-out-of-three match—by the score of 6–3. I could see Ron was a little flustered, and although he'd never really reacted this way before when he got behind, I could understand how he felt. This was, after all, a tournament. But I really wasn't prepared for what happened in the second set. Ron started cheating! Now I know this is a terrible thing to say about someone, particularly a friend, but there's no other way to put it. I distinctly lost two aces in one game, and there were all kinds of other calls that were flagrant cheating. No doubt about it. I didn't know what to do, except keep playing, which I did. I eventually won in three sets, but it took me a while to get over the episode and to play Ron informally again. And you know what happened when I did? He played as honest as a judge."

Ron is a thirty-seven-year-old draftsman whose side of the match contains little of the outer-directed animosity that does Del's.

"Yeah, Del beat me. Not to take anything away from him, but I blew it. I don't know what happened. Maybe I was overconfident because I almost always beat him. I was sort of glad the draw worked out the way it did, because I figured it would give me the best of both worlds: I'd get into the next round of the tournament, and I'd get to play someone new. As a matter of fact, I knew damn well I could beat either one of the guys I would have played in the second round, and that would have put me in the quarter finals. But I got behind early against Del and I couldn't seem to catch up. By the time I discovered I was in a real match, I guess it was too late. I played all right in the second and third sets, but Del seemed to play better, too. It's really funny, because I played him about a month after that and beat him something like 6–2, 6–2."

Strange. Ron makes no mention of having cheated. Indeed, he may not have, but it seems unlikely that Del—who loses to Ron more often than not—would make such an accusation after having beaten him. Let's assume for a moment that Ron did cheat. Is he hiding it from us? Perhaps. More likely is the fact Ron *wanted* Del's shots to be out so badly that he unconsciously saw them as out, and called them that way, without realizing what he was doing. "I always beat him," he told us without qualification. He also planned to "get into the next round of the tournament" rather easily. But something began to go wrong. Del began to play a bit better than usual, Ron a little worse. And Ron, whose expectations of victory and advancement weren't being met, unknowingly began to call on something else: cheating.

It's not that Ron was seeking perfection, which most adults

realize is an unattainable goal. Instead, he was trying to live up to his image of his ideal self, which in this case was capable of easily defeating Del and moving forward in the tournament. When Del began threatening his self-esteem by pulling ahead in the match, Ron resorted to a few unconscious white lies—well-intentioned untruths. As happens to so many tennis players, he wasn't able to tolerate his failure to achieve his ideal. Some people simply have a difficult time accepting who they are and dealing with their own limitations both on and off the court. Others may go so far as to be completely intolerant of their own imperfections, always striving for some vague unattainable power and complete mastery. Ron doesn't sound like such a rivalrous seeker of God-like glories, but it's evident he used cheating to keep his self-esteem from plummeting. Ironically, it seems to have spurred Del to greater heights. A person who has little need to cheat is probably someone who has a good sense of self-worth. He or she is realistic about personal shortcomings. The images of the ideal self and the actual self are close together.

But if self-esteem is heavily entwined with cheating, so is it meshed with another aspect of tennis. This is a more mysterious tendency, and one that is discussed on or about the courts in tones no less hushed than is cheating itself. It is anticipated with all the pleasure of a visit from the Internal Revenue Service and is generally understood by pro and hacker alike about as well as would be the specifics of interplanetary travel.

We're speaking, of course, of the dreaded *choke*.[5]

Even the language is misunderstood. *To choke,* which is defined in one dictionary as "to fail to perform effectively because of nervous agitation or tension," has incorrectly become synonymous with *to clutch*. This is an inaccuracy proba-

---

[5] We'll deal with the hacker, since the pro undoubtedly operates under somewhat different pressures than the rest of us. Nevertheless, it's interesting to note that both pros and hackers tend to choke at similar moments in a game.

bly brought about by the term *in the clutch*, which means "in a tense or perilous situation." Thus, one most often *"chokes in the clutch,"* that is, fails to perform effectively in a particularly tense situation. Mark Edmonds, who in 1976 became the only unseeded player ever to win the Australian Open singles title, once explained the difference between the average professional (himself) and the consistent winner: "The difference between them and us was that at 30–40 on the other bloke's serve we hit into the net and they didn't." [6] Or, put another way, choking means playing tennis worst when it means most.

Of course, just when "it means most" depends on the individual player. Choking might grip you at match point. It might rear its head during a set played against someone you particularly want to beat, or while you are performing in front of somebody you specifically want to impress. Maybe a large audience is watching, or just a single person (but one who is important to you). Whatever the case, choking seems to be linked to an acute awareness—whether conscious or unconcious—that your tennis circumstances are no longer ordinary.

Debbi, for instance, recently experienced a choke in the clutch. She is a twenty-six-year-old administrative assistant to the president of a food company and has been playing competitive tennis since entering college, eight years ago.

"But believe it or not, in all that time I've never gotten to the finals of a tournament. At least not in singles. I played on the women's team at the university, but that was more a team sport than an individual one. And I did win a local doubles tournament a couple of years ago with a really terrific player as my partner. So when I found myself in the finals of a club tournament a month or so ago, you can imagine why I wasn't all that prepared for it. The first thing I noticed when I walked out onto the court for the match was that a lot of the members had come over from the bar to watch us play. The fact that I knew a lot of them made me very uneasy. And the fact that my opponent was the number-one seed didn't do much for

[6] *World Tennis*, April 1976.

my composure either. The whole thing was a disaster. I don't know, my mind just seemed to go numb or something. When play started, I was afraid to try anything chancy and just tried to keep it safe. Which, I should add, is no way to play this particular woman. She's a vulture if she gets to the net. I just didn't start playing my game until it was too late. By then we were halfway through the second set and it was all over."

What Debbi says about not "playing my game" is extremely important. That's what choking does. It throws molasses into the smoothly functioning tennis gears. The muscles seem to freeze temporarily, and until they thaw there is a feeling of thorough disorganization. So it is vital to realize that a connection exists between *muscle tension* and *mind tension*. People who are anxious have tense muscles, which in turn cause them to hit the ball short and set up an opponent. What was once firm, steady play becomes tentative and erratic.

Since choking tends to occur "in the clutch," it is apparent that the choker has some sense of the presence of "the clutch," whether consciously or subconsciously. In other words, he knows or feels that this is a "tense and perilous situation" for him. Choking is not a random accident, nor is it to be confused with the more temporary "psyche-out" described in Chapter 9.

But what is really happening? Why the tendency to feel "tight" when choking? For one thing, apprehension or outright fear of a particular situation can lead to massive inhibition, as well as to an apparent regression. Beset with stress, it is not unusual for people to return to early modes of behavior and to forget what they've learned more recently. To many players this means reverting to the cautious style of game they first played. They begin to "play it safe," attempting only what they think they can get away with (old), while forgetting anything vaguely risky (new). Fear of making a mistake leads to the quest for security. Suddenly they are no longer capable of playing loosely or of playing "their game." Mental and physical paralysis caused by anxiety have combined to corral their sense of freedom and make their styles hesitant and error-prone. They have *choked in the clutch.*

Like the motives for cheating, the reasons for choking are related to specific players. We explained in Chapter 3 how tennis can legitimize aggression, how the guilt that frequently accompanies the notion of taking the offensive may be by-passed through an overhead smash made within strict bounds, freeing the player to experience almost sensuous pleasure and emotional relief: tennis as *permission.* But we also showed that there are times when a player senses that he or she has strained personal limits or transgressed the prerogatives of others. Guilt arises. People feel they have gone too far. They become self-conscious. This is frequently what leads to the choke.

Take the case of Ray, a middle-aged college professor and a pretty good tennis player.

"I was playing a good friend, a psychiatrist as a matter of fact, who's my age. I played him fairly well for a while, rushing the net a lot, and I had him 5–2, 40–love. Set point. When I went to serve, I know I said to myself, 'guaranteed double fault.' And sure enough, that's exactly what I did. I went on to lose that game, and the next four games, and to lose the set, 7–5. I've thought about what happened, and I think I had this feeling that 'it could have been me' over there getting beaten so badly. I think it had something to do with our relative ages and professions because I had about the same situation with a younger fellow a while later and I won without any problem."

Ray is perceptive. He realizes that *whom* he was playing —as well as some overly empathetic feeling of identification— may have caused him to choke. Most people understand the fear of failure; but what's deeper than that, and more difficult to comprehend, is the fear that many people have of *success,* particularly against certain persons. They subconsciously prefer to lose. "Champions are afraid to lose," Billie Jean King has said, "when most others are *afraid to win.*" [7] Triumph—particularly when perceived as causing the annihilation of someone real or imagined—can produce self-consciousness, fear, and anxiety. That's when mind tension = muscle tension = choke. In Ray's case, he was protecting himself. Another player, who has, say, many unresolved feelings toward a dead parent, may choke when confronted by an older player. Another may fantasize that an opponent is a younger sister toward whom he or she always felt protective. Rather than annihilate such figures, players may choose to destroy themselves instead by suddenly backing off and losing.

What success might mean to the *self* as well as to others can also cause choking. For many people the feeling of *grandiosity* that can accompany winning by too large a margin is more than they can stand. To them the grandeur they believe must inevitably accompany total victory is dangerous. They fear it may be despised by others. A 6–0 win is perceived as a one-way ticket out of a milieu where everybody's chummy. Further, some of these players may be subconsciously afraid that such a victory might release overt childish glee and consequent shame. They are afraid that if they get too close to the white heat of greatness they will—like Icarus—be cruising for a fall. Better to remain grounded than to risk the flight.

And, of course, you can never be knocked down if you never get up. Some players just can't go for "the kill" because they're afraid of being "killed" themselves. They fear the retaliation they imagine to be unavoidable should they release the aggression that threatens to destroy an opponent. Surely some force awaits them, they feel, ready to pounce should they succeed. The "will to fail" marches on.

These examples describe the *emotional* self-consciousness that sometimes wells up inside a player and causes him or her to choke. There is also a more *intellectual* type of self-

[7] *The New York Times*, January 14, 1976, p. 46 (italics ours).

consciousness at work. Mary, a forty-eight-year-old educational consultant who has been a tennis player on and off since her youth, knows this well.

"These days I'm playing twice a week, and a rather remarkable thing has happened. For some reason, the women I play with on Fridays have decided to put a little wager on the game. A grand total of one dollar. My Monday game, meanwhile, is strictly a no-bet affair. Well, the difference in how I play on the two days is unbelievable. No matter how silly it sounds to you, I play much worse with that crummy dollar on the line than I do when nothing's at stake. And no matter how much I tell myself that I'm playing badly because of the dollar—or because I'm thinking too much—my game doesn't improve. That's when I start thinking too much about thinking too much, if you know what I mean. I know if we'd just call off the bet we'd probably all play better. My God, can you imagine how we'd play with $20,000 on the line like the pros?"

What happens to Mary happens to many tennis players: a distraction leads to too much mechanical and analytical thinking, and too much thinking about mechanics and analysis. It seems almost as if the right hemisphere of the brain—the more emotional, artistic, and spatially oriented side—has fallen further under the influence of the usually dominant left hemisphere, which is more verbal and analytical. Recent studies on children indicate that those who are heavily left-dominated may be so verbally analytical that they can be hindered when it comes to such things as copying a tennis serve. Notice what happens to many tennis players immediately after taking lessons. They analyze and verbalize their shot making, and in "going by the book" they give themselves vast numbers of instructions to follow. "Feet eighteen inches apart; shorten your backswing; bend the knees; keep the wrist firm; use the Eastern grip with the index finger forward. . . ." The players' minds are bundles of calculations, reminders, and judgments. The result is usually a depressing downward trend in ability which slowly disappears as the brain becomes less analytical and more freewheeling. Mary began to think too much about her shot making, not because she'd just taken lessons, but because a somewhat similar external seduction—the bet—added weight to her shots. Hers is a classic case of "trying too hard." In her awareness of this she managed to achieve a state of supreme irony: "*trying* to *relax.*"

There are many players who ultimately combine the worst of these emotional and rational worlds. Unlike the majority of cheaters—who are trying to keep their precarious self-esteem from falling—certain chokers may be suffering from some form of too much ego. Take the players for whom an audience is a cue to fall apart, for instance. This is their private version of being in the clutch. It ordinarily takes considerable confidence or exhibitionism to believe that many people would actually drop everything to watch one play. For most, self-consciousness is tremendously heightened by the belief that they hold center stage. This is an *emotional* state which may lead to too *intellectual* a response. Imagining the klieg lights to be burning brightly, these players suddenly begin to "try too hard." They start giving instructions to themselves. Too much thinking simply confuses and immobilizes them. They freeze. Their normal game—"*their game*"—is gone.

If you happen to discover a sure cure for choking on the tennis court, rest assured that there is a market of thirty-odd million people waiting to buy it at any price. Unfortunately, what might be a good prescription for one patient might not work for another. In reality, the road to eliminating much of the choking and cheating we see in tennis runs through the integration of self discussed at the end of Chapter 2. "Pulling yourself together" on the court means organizing and balancing both your aggression and your self-esteem to the point where you are least anxious and therefore least self-conscious. While concentration is the key, it is being continually inter-

rupted by outside issues with very personal emotional implications. Debbi is worried about winning a tournament in front
of her friends. Ray is inhibited about thrashing someone in
whom he sees much of himself. Mary can't get a dollar bill out
of her mind. All three realize they're off their game because
they don't *feel like themselves.* Cheating and choking both
contain elements that are linked to self-esteem. More importantly, both show what can happen when players aren't "mentally together."

SEVEN WAYS TO NET PROFIT

1. *Read and familiarize yourself with the Code of the United
States Tennis Association (USTA).* This is distinctly different from
the rules of the game and presents the written unwritten code of
ethics. It can stop problems before they begin and is available for 50
cents from USTA Publications, 71 University Place, Princeton, New
Jersey 08540.

2. *Don't treat cheating as if it didn't exist.* Caught up in the
pristine nature of tennis, many players view cheating as something
best ignored. This is frequently a mistake. If you believe someone is
not making calls correctly—or if you think you may be doing this
yourself—politely get the subject out in the open with opponents
and partners. They're probably as concerned about it as you are.

3. *If you're cheating, ask yourself if it's really worth it.* No moral-
izing here. But cheating can hurt your game in three ways. First, it
can incite your opponent to better things. Second, it can turn you
into an average guilt-ridden American tennis player, which is bound
to inhibit your shot making. Third, for every point gained cheating,
two may be lost by guilt. In the end you may lose more points than
you gain.

4. *Recognize the humiliation that frequently leads to cheating.*
Part of changing a condition is the willingness to name it and trace
its roots. If you can identify moments of humiliation—both for yourself and for opponents—you will begin to understand why cheating
occurs on the courts.

5. *When you feel you've been cheated, direct your aggression*

back across the net, rather than inward. Tendencies to take cheating personally, to feel sorry for yourself, to blow your stack, or to simmer in righteous indignation won't help your game at all. On the other hand, giving yourself permission to be aggressive could improve your shots enormously.

6. *Remind yourself that it's O.K. to win.* The fear of success is inside more tennis players than you think. If you feel a choke coming on, try consciously telling yourself that there's nothing wrong with winning and that you can't possibly hurt that person across the net.

7. *Play each point as a separate entity, not within a larger context.* Most people are at least subconsciously aware that they are "in the clutch," or a tense situation. But if individual points can be separated from the game as a whole, "the clutch" ceases to exist. Every point means the same thing. So play them one at a time.

7

Advantage, Women?

Cast study: GRACE, age 34

Grace has been playing tennis for more than ten years. Although she's never reached the "A" level in the various clubs to which she's belonged, she has always been considered a solid "B" player who could be counted on to provide a consistent game during the one or two times she played each week. She gave up the sport during a recent pregnancy—her first—but returned to play better than ever. More recently, though, Grace has been in what she calls "a perfectly disastrous slump." She has been repeatedly netting even the easiest of shots, while both her mind and her body have been wandering around the court without any apparent direction whatsoever.

Unlike most players who undergo a sudden such transformation, Grace believes she can pinpoint its origins. During analysis she explained how it all began. It seems she was attending a cocktail party a few days after having scored a pair of upsets in the first two rounds of a club doubles tournament. While at the party she was commenting to a non-tennis-playing male acquaintance that the victories had been particularly satisfying. "I suspect," replied the friend, "that tennis is a terrific way to let out your aggression." Grace was startled by the seemingly harmless statement. "My God," she thought, "he's right." The comment stayed with her for days, and when the next round of the tournament began, she couldn't drive it from her mind. She played terribly after a fair start, and she and her partner lost after a long and tedious struggle. Worse, she has continued to play poorly for the past few weeks. The offhand cocktail party remark still haunts her.

114

Obviously, it is the notion of being openly aggressive that is bothering Grace. She was raised in lower-middle-class surroundings, the oldest of two daughters of a woman who doted on an alcoholic and unemployable husband. She hated her father and could never understand why her mother tolerated his alternating moods of rowdiness and inertia. She was also hostile toward her sister, whom she felt her mother favored as well. Jealousy would often bubble up inside her to the point where she would have fantasies that both her sister and her father were dead, and the vision came stunningly true during her teens: the sister drowned during a school outing when Grace was fifteen, and the father died of a protracted liver ailment a year later. It seemed to Grace that her wishes must certainly have had something to do with what happened.

She eventually went to college, earned a master's degree, married, and had her first child. In analysis she frequently dwelled upon the aggression that seethed inside her toward her father and sister. It is obvious she still feels guilty about them, believing that she somehow contributed to their deaths through her jealousy. As a result she is extremely fearful of causing harm to others. She knows she has the capacity to be aggressive but desperately wants to keep a tight rein on such tendencies. Thus, when someone harmlessly suggested that she was "letting out her aggression" on the tennis court, she was unable to function.

"When that comment was made to me," she recalls, "it made me stop and think about tennis. I asked myself, 'Is this the way you really want to act?' I know part of the problem is the feelings I have about my father and sister. I've thought about that. But there's more. Tennis must be more difficult for a woman than a man. No one tells girls they can have an outlet for their aggression. They're always expected to meet people and be pleasant. Most of the time I'm being a mother, I'm nourishing, I take care of my baby, and then suddenly I'm supposed to be aggressive. Well, I don't want to hate anybody, on the tennis court or anywhere else."

Tennis may have been traditionally considered "a gentleman's game," [1] but during the 1970s it has cashed in hand-

[1] Odd, since Major Walter C. Wingfield invented the sport expressly to provide a means of outdoor exercise for his lady friends.

somely on the concept of feminism. Female professional tennis has become a solid sell, mixing commercialism with womanhood to create the first authentic collection of sports heroines in the country's history. Prior to this phenomenon it was only the occasional woman athlete who captured the nation's imagination, while often collecting aspersions on her femininity as well. Babe Zaharias and Althea Gibson were once considered oddballs in many quarters; Billie Jean and Chrissie are slowly becoming role models equal to Kareem and Catfish.

If we think in terms of tax brackets, they have already achieved such heights. When the first Virginia Slims tournament was played in Houston in 1970, the winner took home $1,600 out of the $7,500 prize money anted up by the Philip Morris Company. By 1976 ten such tournaments were each offering $75,000 to participants, with weekly winners cashing checks for $15,000. A year earlier Chris Evert earned more money—$352,227—than any male tennis player.[2] Perhaps the women's professional tour does not have the depth of its male counterpart, but it certainly has all the color and most of the respectability.

Considering that highly competitive sports have always been deemed "unfeminine" in America, this is no mean feat. The macho tradition runs deep, and the conflict between being an athlete and being a girl has usually been resolved in favor of the latter. Women were not *supposed* to be jocks, and if they somehow found their way onto a golf course or cinder track, they were automatically considered inferior to their male counterparts. The apex of a young girl's athletic achievement was to be told that she could "hit and throw like a boy," and she was expected eventually to stop such nonsense and get on with being "ladylike." When, during the early 1950s, General Douglas MacArthur suggested that "fathers and

[2] But female pros have not yet reached equal pay; the average "Top Ten" woman player earned 63 percent of what the "Top Ten" male earned in 1975.

mothers who would have their sons be men should have them participate in sports," it was no accident that he ignored more than half the nation's population. Obviously, increasing interest in feminism has altered this view to some degree during the last few years, particularly among younger women. More and more of them, for instance, are participating in formal college athletics, spurred on by federal legislation.[3] But it would be a mistake to think that tennis at this time is not unique in producing a number of $100,000-a-year female athletes.

As for the "average" woman, her place seems to be on the court. It follows. When increased consciousness raising is combined with increased news media coverage, the result is bound to be flocks of women of all ages imagining themselves capable of duplicating the gazelle-like stars they see leaping across their television screens. It seems safe to say that no other sport in the United States is currently being played by so many females. Women, in fact, may soon outnumber men on the courts.

However, even the most ardent of women's liberationists would not claim total similarity between what have come to be called "men's tennis" and "women's tennis." It is our own feeling that women and men are more alike than not in the way they play the game, but there are also significant differences. Whether these dissimilarities are cultural, biological, or psychological in origin remains to be seen in many cases. But based on our experiences with patients and discussions with other female players, there appears to be little doubt that women experience a somewhat different set of circumstances on the court than do men.

Part of this is physical. As Grace Lichtenstein, a *New York Times* reporter who followed the women's professional tour

---

[3] Title IX was a controversial part of the federal Education Amendments Act of 1972, a manifesto that prohibited discrimination on the basis of sex in college athletic programs that receive federal funds or other federal assistance.

and wrote a book [4] about what she found, puts it: "The men were bigger and stronger than the women, just as heavyweights were bigger and stronger than featherweights." Men's tennis is thought of as a rapid-paced, kill-or-be-killed, serve-and-volley game. Women's tennis is considered to have more of a slowly paced, wait-and-see, baseline-to-baseline style. (There are obviously many exceptions to this. A match pitting Rosie Casals against the guy next door would be one of them.) Many women simply do not have the strength to serve and get to the net before the return catches them in what is somewhat inaccurately referred to as "no-man's land." In two surveys undertaken by *Tennis* magazine in 1974 and 1975,[5] it was found that the speed of the fastest male serve (that of Colin Dibley) was 148 miles per hour, while the fastest female serve (Margaret Court's) was clocked at 92.6 miles per hour. Average for the top eight men was 137 miles per hour, while the figure for the best eight women was 88.9 miles per hour—indicating that professional women players serve at roughly two-thirds the speed of their male counterparts.

The female skeleton is lighter and smaller than the male as a rule, and while this is not necessarily related to physical strength, it does appear that men are stronger than women for at least the first two-thirds of life. One study [6] indicates that while women are typically weaker overall than men when tested for absolute strength, they are more so in upper body strength (where they are 43 to 63 percent weaker) than in lower body strength (27 percent weaker). This would seem to indicate that they compare more favorably with men when they undertake activities they normally share such as walking and climbing stairs. Women don't use their upper bodies to the extent that men do. Further, the motor performances of

[4] Grace Lichtenstein, *A Long Way, Baby* (New York: William Morrow, 1974).

[5] *Tennis*, November 1974, pp. 23–27; April 1975, pp. 36–39.

[6] Jack H. Wilmore, "Inferiority of the Female Athlete: Myth or Reality?" *Rx Sports and Travel*, March–April 1975.

girls are generally considered to be as strong as those of boys until both reach about age thirteen, whereupon the motor performances of girls tend to level off (at just about the time there's pressure on them to be "ladylike"), while those of boys continue to increase. This suggests that at least part of the gap is cultural or social, and that with more emphasis on women's athletics the strength differences between the sexes may lessen. Of course, there are simply certain situations that women will never share with men: many tennis-playing females report that their timing is off during their menstrual periods, while others mention feeling disoriented during early stages of pregnancy.

Nevertheless, our impression is that there are more "tennis junkies" [7] among women than men. One reason for this may be the amount of leisure time society has heretofore granted women. This is particularly true for older married females who feel their skills are not marketable. Often their children have grown up and left home, and many of them sense a void that needs filling. Tennis becomes a way to achieve a sense of self-worth and of belonging to something amid the wasteland of coffee klatches and card parties that the life of the American "housewife" can become. Even younger mothers who have given up careers and are raising children may end up asking themselves, "Is that all there is?" Tennis becomes a way to compensate for the things they feel they're missing in a "man's world." It's one of the great equalizers.

Jane, for example, is a thirty-seven-year-old mother of two sons who started playing tennis about three years ago.

"To say that tennis has taken over my life would probably be an understatement. I do my shopping with a raincoat over my tennis

---

[7] A "tennis junkie" is just what it sounds like: someone who's hopelessly addicted to tennis. Symptoms include playing once, and sometimes even twice, every day, as well as talking tennis at all hours of the day or night. The habit is difficult to kick, particularly in advanced stages.

dress, and I arrange to drive the boys to and from school around my matches. When I started out, I was a low 'C' player. But I worked my way up the ladder, and today I'm getting near the top of the 'B's. I challenge people above me on the ladder every chance I get. It's sort of a joke around the club that you'd better look over your shoulder because I might be creeping up on you! This year I'm in charge of the women's tournaments: seeding, making up draw sheets, arranging matches, and things like that. I know it sounds like a cliché to say that tennis gives me something to do while the boys are at school, but I'm afraid it's true. I like to be active, to organize things, and that's what I'm doing. My husband doesn't play, and with what I've seen of mixed doubles, that's fine with me. Besides, I think of tennis as my game, not his."

Jane's story is a common one. The rigid outline of tennis and its culture makes the game particularly attractive to someone who wants to feel purposeful. Advancement and success are both rapid and obvious, especially for beginners. Tennis clubs are much like corporate structures, with their own little hierarchies to which lesser players aspire. These "junior executives" receive promotions if they do well, moving up a rung or two to play with a higher caliber of opponent, or being placed in charge of arrangements. They acquire recognition, status, and power. As was pointed out in Chapter 1, the very organization found in tennis makes it of interest to many people. For women, many of whom have been excluded from the highly organized world of business, it provides a particularly comforting climate.

Are there deeper psychological reasons why women may tend to be more attracted to heavy doses of tennis than are men? One answer may revolve around the fact that very often much of a woman's life is spent trying to work out her relationship with her father (just as a man's strongest emotional challenges may primarily involve his mother). For many women there is a strong need for love from the father figure, who comes to represent authority. He becomes a living symbol of rules and regulations. As youngsters, girls therefore tend to show more respect for obedience and regulations than boys. They are less rebellious and more compliant. They are frequently better behaved in school. In this respect, the gentility of tennis almost makes the game "feminine." Indeed, we are not far removed from the days when it was considered a "sissy sport" because of its premium on conforming behavior.

Further, some girls always feel the need to be the athletic sons their fathers never had or to make up for sons who never amounted to anything. At the same time, many a father makes clear to his daughter from the first moment she clutches a racquet that they possess a special on-court relationship that she should preserve for the rest of her life. For a host of reasons these girls always feel they can please their fathers more easily than their mothers. This appears to be quite common among women tennis professionals.

According to Jane and others we've interviewed, women's amateur tennis leagues tend to be less casual than men's. Matches seem to be taken more seriously, while the sense of emotional hurt lasts longer. This would seem to be borne out by observations that female professionals react to the game more emotionally than do their counterparts on the men's tour. Of course claiming that women are more subject to emotional interference on the tennis court smacks of the old chauvinistic chestnut: "They're always crying about something." It could be argued in response that many women are simply conforming to what they've been told is appropriate female behavior.

Nevertheless, the fact remains that our culture has provided women with greater latitude for expressing emotion, no matter what its motives in doing so. Men, on the other hand, are trained to remain cool and collected and to provide the steady shoulder on which the sweet young thing may cry. And God forbid that a man should himself cry in public. The male ethic steadfastly proclaims that Thou Shalt Not Complain Whilst Losing, while it is still considered acceptable for a woman to make excuses. Like the concept of female compliance with authority, these are emotional roles for which the basic training begins early in life. For example, psychoanalyst Erik Erikson found [8] in one experiment that the play scenes created by girls age eleven through thirteen tend to be quiet and inner-directed. The girls created peaceful family constellations. Those scenes invented by boys, however, were noisy and outer-directed. This suggests that when game playing, women may be more in touch with their emotions than men. As a result they may often feel more of a willingness to take the results of a tennis game to heart. Indeed, there seems to be more fierceness and rivalry among women, more a feeling that it's all personal and less a game.

But the high emotional level of tennis as played by many women shouldn't be confused with *aggression*. For if some females are raised with respect for authority while being granted permission to display emotions openly, so are they traditionally taught in no uncertain terms that they are not the aggressive sex on this planet. Naturally this has all sorts of ramifications when they decide to take up tennis, as it eventually had for Grace, who as we saw at the beginning of this chapter was in a state of anxiety over abruptly realizing that the game contained more aggression than she realized. There is also the case of Chris, a middle-aged player who recently trundled her so-so game off to tennis camp and made an equally startling, though completely opposite, discovery.

"Essentially, I've always had trouble being aggressive on the court. I wasn't terribly athletic growing up, and even if I had been, I would have been limited to field hockey. That's what 'girls' gym' was in those days: strap on a couple of shin guards and run around in rather unshort short shorts while gently poking at each other

[8] Erik H. Erikson, "Sex Differences in the Play Configurations of Preadolescents," *American Journal of Orthopsychiatry* 21 (October 1951).

with sticks. The idea of a girl taking lessons at anything more strenuous than the piano or ballroom dancing was considered improper.
So when I started playing tennis, it was like learning a new language. I'd watch these women on TV and it would look so easy, but
I just couldn't hit the ball very hard. And I never learned how to
volley because I never got close enough to the net, not even in
doubles. Anyway, I packed myself off to tennis camp last year and
went through the first two days with almost no change. Then one of
the instructors told me that I should think 'Kill!' every time I hit the
ball. I thought it was pretty stupid to be running around the court
thinking of murder and mayhem, but he kept after me until I finally
tried it. Well, the difference was absolutely incredible. 'Kill! Kill!
Kill!' Suddenly I was hitting the ball twice as hard as before. Literally. As soon as I stopped saying it to myself, I'd go back to patty-
caking. I paid almost $400 for the camp, and if that's the only thing I
learned, it was worth it."

Even allowing for factors of strength, it is clear that overt
aggression has not been included in the lexicon of most
women, particularly those over thirty-five years of age. On
the whole they have been schooled to be nonaggressive, although there are geographic and ethnic differences. (A
woman raised on the sun-drenched public playgrounds of
southern California is probably going to have more training in
aggression than a lady reared in an antebellum atmosphere
down South.) Even that most liberal of baby doctors, Dr.
Benjamin Spock, once warned a generation of parents that
"when women are encouraged to be competitive too many of
them become disagreeable." [9] In trailing the world's best female players, Grace Lichtenstein found they were well aware
of the necessity of "killer instinct." "And yet," she wrote, "undoubtedly because they were women, they voiced fears about
what that instinct might do to them." [10]

[9] Benjamin Spock, *Decent and Indecent—Our Personal and Political Behavior*
(New York: McCall, 1970), p. 47.

[10] Lichtenstein, *A Long Way, Baby*, p. 97.

If the best players in the world are anxious about displaying their aggression, imagine what is happening inside the hearts and minds of many a female hacker. One of them told us:

"It's like entering an arena where you're not supposed to be. It's like you don't know the rules. It's not so much that winning is bad. It's like if you're being aggressive you're in a foreign country. You don't know how to be aggressive, and when to stop. Or even if it's nice to be aggressive. There's a whole vocabulary that women haven't been included in."

Ironically, this is what makes tennis junkies out of many women. The court issues them a license that society does not. It provides a regular "fix" which the nontennis world won't yet tolerate. The more we've talked to female players, the more we've been impressed by the vacuum that tennis has apparently filled for many of them. While culture demands that they be submissive, tennis allows them to let it all hang out. Sometimes the need to do this is obscure—in Chapter 1 we saw that Sheila had become a very aggressive player after noting somewhat resentfully, "The house is empty almost every day, so why stay home?" At other times players know precisely what the game means to them—in Chapter 3 we noted that Janet realized full well her motives for bolting from the house and hitting balls off a brick wall until she "literally tore the covers off." The problem comes when women don't feel comfortable with aggression off or on the court. Grace, whom we saw at the beginning of this chapter trying to deal with her new role as a mother, is obviously having trouble. Chris, whom we just met, is not. As the American pendulum swings from the former to the latter—pushed by society and legislation—more and more women may find themselves able to think "Kill! Kill! Kill!" on the tennis court. They will be able to bind their aggression, to release it in a situation controlled by fixed rules and lines. Matters of strength aside, hell hath no fury like a woman finally given permission to smack the living fuzz off a tennis ball.

But lacking the will to kill is only part of the problem. *Receiving* aggression can be as difficult for women as handling a slice serve with a quick kick. Because many females have been brought up to believe that they're immune from attack of any sort, they naturally assume they'll have protection on the court. Someone has always been looking out for them, many of them figure, and why should things be any different now? Nothing could be more damaging, particularly in singles. You're all alone out there, and cringing at the baseline is a losing strategy. It's no accident that we've found women far more concerned about getting physically injured than men.

Not only do they prefer to avoid physical attack, but some females take another step down the ladder of aggression with their inability to cope with outbursts of anger by opponents and partners. They recoil at such displays, whether or not the fireworks represent criticisms of their own play. A short fuse on a partner is a particular danger. By turning inward when it ignites—and refusing to let aggression flow outward in the form of "fighting back"—they respond with an inner, trapped rage which sometimes results in tears.

Actually, there *are* singular moments when many women feel free to be totally aggressive—at least temporarily. Notwithstanding the failure of Margaret Court against Bobby Riggs in 1973 (and the inability of particular women to play well against particular men for whatever reason), these periods of aggression often arrive when the person on the other side of the net is male. Aha, you are saying: the innate battle of the sexes. Actually, yes and no. Most competitive sports, following society's lead, separate the sexes. The desire to be with one's own kind, physically speaking, is a potent force. The tendency is for men to gather with men and women with women, and tennis respects the dividing lines. However, the two sexes *do* sometimes get together as oppo-

nents, and most of the women to whom we've talked reflect
the opinion of Betty, a player in her mid-thirties who was
raised on a year-round diet of tennis.

"I'm really relaxed when I play a man. The same thing happens
when I play certain women who are better than I am. The reason, to
me, seems clear. I know that I can go out and play hard, but no one
really expects me to win. There's no risk for me or for any other
woman who goes out there against a man. It's O.K. to lose to the
man. That's the way it's always been. So the outcome of the aggression is understood: the man is going to win. I think I'd much rather
play men because all the fear of failure is gone."

Betty's comfortable style, when she plays men, is battling
and perhaps even snuffing out her tennis tensions. Her reduced expectations fend off much potential disappointment.
But it's also interesting to see just what happens to another
woman when she actually starts *beating* a man. This is Cindy,
who is a forty-seven-year-old psychologist and has been playing tennis for more than twenty years.

"The best way to explain it is to tell you what happened recently
when I played an old friend who'd come into town for a few days.
I'd never seen him play before, and when we got on the court to
warm up it was obvious he wasn't very good. I knew right away that
I could beat him. You know how you can sometimes tell after only
two or three shots? We started to play a set, and I won the first
three games rather easily. I could see he was embarrassed by what
was happening, and I felt bad, too. I was asking myself, 'Gosh,
should I really beat him? He's going to feel terrible if he loses to a
woman.' Right at that point, I began to lose. I tried to psyche myself
up by saying it was all right to beat a man, but I knew damn well
that I would rather lose to this guy. I've never beaten a man, and
beating him was confusing. We never finished the set because
some friends came along and we were able to play doubles, but I
knew he was relieved to have caught up in our match. And I was relieved, too."

At this moment in history it seems that many women feel more comfortable playing men *until they begin to win.* Like Betty, they initially sense that the pressure is off because no one really expects them to do well—least of all themselves. But, like Cindy, when they get ahead they experience a particularly female version of the choke: fear of success against men brought about by conditioning. "Beating him was confusing" for Cindy because it meant such a stark reversal of roles. Society has dictated that the male is to be aggressive, the female submissive. While this view is being altered by many younger women, who, as one of them told us, just love to smash a ball at a man, females of Cindy's generation have a difficult time overcoming what they've been coerced into believing for years. When Margaret Court lost to Bobby Riggs in 1973, it wasn't because she didn't make the shots; it was because, given her relationship with men, she *couldn't* make the shots. Billie Jean King, who beat Riggs shortly thereafter, has a decidedly different view of men. While Court is probably more typical, King represents the change that is very slowly taking place.

Another striking example of the difficulty women can have beating men turned up in 1976, when a transsexual by the name of Dr. Renee Richards entered a number of women's professional tournaments. A one-time male player of minor note, Richards caused a stir among the females who suddenly found themselves across the net from someone they still perceived as a man. One of them, Cathy Beene, "said her problems began when she knew she could win," according to *The New York Times.*[11] The *Times* continued: " 'The first game I wasn't nervous,' the 24-year-old Texan said of her opening women's singles match against Renee Richards in the $60,000 Tennis Week Open at Orange Tennis Club today. 'Then when I realized I could beat her, I got nervous.' "

(It does appear, however, that one way "love" literally

[11] *The New York Times*, August 22, 1976, section 5, p. 1.

enters tennis is through the door clearly marked "Eros."
Many women are aware that they have the wherewithal to
distract men, at least more than the reverse is true. One
woman told us that brushing up against a male opponent
while changing ends between games is a method guaranteed
to win the next five points. Another proudly announced,
"Whenever I play against a man I always wear my lace tennis
panties.")

Men, meanwhile, are hardly absolved from playing locked-
in on-court roles vis-à-vis women. We know one male who
lost to a woman and came off the court with the announcement that he "let" her win. Fat chance. Cindy, in perceiving
that a man "is going to feel terrible if he loses to a woman," is
dead right. Take what happened to Chuck, a computer pro-
grammer. At age forty-three he thought he had played
enough tennis to deal with almost anything on the court.

"But I wasn't prepared for playing Helen. She'd always been considered one of the top gal players in our club, and she sure hangs
around the place enough to be good. So when my regular opponent didn't show up one Saturday, there she was, looking for someone to play with. I figured, what the hell. We went out on the courts
and began hitting next to a foursome of guys whom I played with
once in a while. So when they saw me with her, a couple of them
began to needle me a little. 'Oh oh,' one of them said, 'looks like
you're in for trouble today. Don't let her beat the pants off you.'
Very funny, right? Well, she did start to beat me. Listen, she's good,
and she plays about twenty-five hours a day. So when these guys
saw she was winning, they really started in on me. Started calling
me 'Riggs' and asking me when I was going to play in the As-
trodome. The more they watched the more I wanted to beat the hell
out of her. And the worse I did, naturally. She was ahead 5–2 when
the bell rang ending the hour, and I practically ran off the court. I
showered at home so I wouldn't have to listen to those jokers in the
locker room."

The man thinks he's *supposed* to win. He's been trained for the power position all his life, and losing can result in total humiliation and anger. Talk about distance between the actual self and the ideal self! Losing to a woman can be a severe blow to fragile self-esteem. Mutilated macho. Further aspersions on her femininity. (Therefore: "I didn't lose to a woman; I lost to a *man*.") Often tennis is a structured little society, complete with its own well-defined classes and subclasses. Everybody has a place. A man losing to a woman is much like an "A" player losing to a "B" player. For the "A" there is a hide-in-the-locker-room loss of pride. For the "B" there can be the uneasy feeling of somehow having broken a rule.

If there's anyone who suffers most from this male/female psychology, it's probably the woman teaching pro. She is a relatively rare species, despite the popularity of the high-dollar professional game and the vast numbers of female hackers roaming the courts. As we've already pointed out, many of her potential female students may be more comfortable playing with men; they believe they have nothing to lose when facing males, and they don't have to feel guilty about their aggression. For a man to take a tennis lesson from a woman means he must admit to her athletic superiority, something his sense of machismo usually won't allow to happen.

For all its appeal to women, tennis remains a thoroughly chauvinistic game. Men often look down upon playing females, or treat them with an overdone sense of chivalry on the court. Hitting a slower service to a female opponent, poaching excessively in front of a woman partner, or heaping excessive praise on even the most forlorn of female wood shots are symptoms left over from the concept of tennis as a "gentleman's game." Or are they? How much, we wonder, is all this simply buffer material to avoid potential humiliation? How many of the jokes about women players are defense mechanisms? If you never play a woman, she can't beat you. If you never serve hard to her, you can always blame her good returns on the fact you "took it easy." Much like the controversy over letting girls into Little League, the *real* fear of females may rest in the vulnerability of the male ego.

The psychological complexities of men and women together on the tennis court are most hellish in that version of the game which is probably the least played and most feared: mixed doubles. Along with "straight doubles" it opens up whole new emotional problems that have nothing to do with returning service crosscourt or playing volleys off your front leg. This is particularly so when partners are husband and wife. There's a whole other mental ball game going on in doubles, multiplied by the simple fact there are twice as many people on the court and the frequent knowledge that some of them are of the opposite sex. As we are about to see, doubles is not necessarily twice the fun.

SEVEN WAYS TO NET PROFIT (for women only)

1. *Expect variations in play with biological changes.* Many women, to one degree or another, experience fluctuations in their games during pregnancy and menstrual periods. These may involve physical discomfort or lack of coordination and timing, but this is perfectly normal. There is even the rare player who performs best during her menstruation.

2. *Don't let the "tennis junkie" syndrome limit your life.* "Shooting up" on tennis is all right to a point. But addiction tends to be all-encompassing. Occasionally, going "cold turkey" for a week or two is a good idea.

3. *Don't allow your lack of strength to convince you that you possess a weak game.* Good tennis involves lots more than simply hitting the ball hard. Lack of physical strength shouldn't prevent a woman from developing other parts of her game to the point where they more than compensate for muscle power.

4. *Issue yourself a license to be aggressive.* It may go against the

grain of this "love" sport (not to mention your basic training as a female), but a little controlled belligerence may help your game. So think offense, not defense, especially if it's not your custom.

5. *Don't be surprised by a display of aggression toward you.* When it comes—and it will—keep your anger directed outward. Don't take criticism to heart. It is far better to *explode* on the ball than to *implode* on yourself.

6. *Don't worry about getting hurt.* More people are injured stepping off the proverbial curb than are hurt on the tennis court. Physically speaking, the worst thing your or anyone else's aggression can cause will probably be no more than a rare bruise.

7. *Don't hesitate to get into a game with men.* Yes, Virginia, you *can* beat him. There is nothing in the rules of tennis that says you can't. If he can't handle defeat by a woman, treat it as his problem, not yours.

8

Doubles Troubles

Case study: JOHN, age 26; ELIZABETH, age 24

Tennis became important at different stages of life for John and Elizabeth, who have been married to each other for four years and have two children. Elizabeth took up the game while attending a proper girls' boarding school on the East Coast, and within a few years she was playing well enough to captain her college team. John started playing more recently, his undergraduate days having been occupied by crew and his early adulthood, by the distractions of arduously pursuing his business career. Lately the two have played the game together with mixed emotional results—as we shall see.

Both John and Elizabeth come from fairly well-to-do families. After college Elizabeth pursued the study of Greek and recently joined the language department of a prestigious university. She is an intelligent, competitive woman who is respected not only for her intellect but also for her capacity for accomplishment. She is just the type of woman to elicit the adjective "sharp" from her acquaintances. John is a rather warm, affable, and easygoing sort, a man who has done well early on in the business world but would not be considered a spectacular success. People think of him in terms of being an "O.K. guy." The couple is extremely popular and welcomed socially into both the academic and business communities. Beneath the solid surface of their union lies a tendency to fall into extremely competitive arguments, but these represent little more than the strains that run through most marriages.

Included in their social life are frequent invitations to play tennis as a doubles team. This, in fact, was one of the reasons John took up the game a few years ago. Elizabeth encouraged him to participate and even promised to teach him, but before long it was evident that there was something wrong with their tennis relationship. More than once the matches fell into verbal disasters filled with criticisms and recriminations. Elizabeth is the more intense of the two, and it seemed as if her professorial nature pushed her into the role of player-coach. John felt humiliated by her "suggestions," which sounded to him more like accusations. Yet she persisted, feeling that she was only trying to help. John usually reacted with countercharges, often asking himself aloud why he had fallen into the clutches of this "castrating bitch." Elizabeth scoffed at such retorts, but it was clear that the outbreaks were no laughing matter to her, John, or their opponents.

In discussing their tennis tensions with each other, the couple finally decided to modify their intense feelings of "togetherness." In fact, they felt it might be best if the two of them no longer played as a team. They began what they laughingly referred to as their "tennis divorce" by asking another couple to split up as well—John was to play with the wife against Elizabeth and the husband. "We're going to get you!" Elizabeth half jokingly called out before the first serve. "Not if we get you first!" John replied. And with that began the most enjoyable ninety minutes of tennis both had played in several months. Elizabeth felt a new fierceness welling up inside her. ("But it was a good feeling," she would later recall. "If my partner made a mistake, I just shrugged it off and got back to the game.") No longer worried that he might be accused of dragging his team down, John found he was able to move to the net with newfound abandon. ("It was like there was a rope pulling me forward. I didn't even have to think about attacking. It just happened.") Not surprisingly, the two found that their best shots were those that were played directly at each other—as if each were finding special pleasure through a private confrontation at the net.

In short, the experiment was a huge success. John and Elizabeth haven't played as a team in months, and their tennis—particularly John's—is greatly improved. More important, they are enjoying each other more away from the court than they did before. "What we tell tennis friends who wonder why we split up on the court," reports John, "is that we had to destroy the team in order to save it."

> TIME: morning, afternoon, or early evening.
> PLACE: any court, U.S.A.

As the scene opens, two young married couples are playing mixed doubles. Their occasional shouts cut through the air, punctuating the repeated sound of ball against racquet. Birds chirp in the nearby trees as sunshine pours over the grainy artificial playing surface. Each member of the foursome appears healthy and relaxed as he or she bounds about the court in apparent harmony, hitting the balls back and forth in yellow brush strokes across the gray-green canvas. This, it would seem, is what tennis is all about: the American dream of achievement and sociability. Except . . .

> Alice keeps deferring to Ted, her partner.
> Ted is trying to hit everything to Jane, his opponent.
> Jane is furious at Tom, her partner.
> Tom wants very much to outshine Ted, his opponent.
> Which is all happening because . . .
> Ted always criticizes Alice for "getting in the way."
> Jane is playing more erratically than Ted.
> Tom and Jane had a fight last night.
> Ted thinks Tom is showing off.

Doubles is a whole new ballgame, filled with its own unique brand of tennis tensions. If singles is like chess in its equality of individual roles, doubles is more like bridge. Now you are *coupled,* and how you play your cards is determined by the hand your partner plays. Doubles is not merely singles multiplied by two, though it is frequently perceived and taught that way. (Indeed, America's tradition of rugged individualism may explain why the country has tended to produce many more top-flight singles players than outstanding doubles teams.) The most obvious differences are physical and strategic. "Singles," Bill Tilden has said, "is essentially a game of speed, punch, brawn; while doubles is a game of position, finesse, subtlety." [1] Doubles requires a less powerful serve and a more accurate return, as well as good volleying and effective lobbing. It takes more patience and planning than singles, which puts a premium on "big shots" and rewards a fondness for going for instant winners.

Doubles is probably the more popular of the two games for at least three reasons. First, it is more social, a kind of tribal rite. Particularly in mixed doubles, the court provides a sort of athletic cocktail party which responds to the need for human companionship. In fact, the tennis courts are fast becoming a stylish version of the singles bar, a respectable place where people can go to advance their sexual concerns without showing too much overt interest. Many tennis clubs organize "singles' doubles nights," and their bulletin boards are often cluttered with "partner wanted" notices that read much like "personal" advertisements in certain newspapers.

Second, doubles is a game that is more suited to older players. Although the 4½-foot-wide doubles alleys tack 700 square feet onto a singles court, playing in a foursome requires that each player be responsible for only two-thirds of the area he or she must cover in singles. Doubles players also—at least in theory—hit only half as many shots as they do playing singles. So there is less strain. As people age, they feel they are taking less of a medical risk by playing doubles, and their fears are not unfounded.

Finally, doubles is a cheaper way to play tennis than is singles, no small factor as the game becomes more and more an indoor product where the right to cream a forehand sells for as much as $50 an hour. And in areas where court space is difficult to come by, having four people play at once makes a great deal of sense.

[1] William T. Tilden, 2d, *Match Play and the Spin of the Ball* (1925; reprint ed., New York: Arno Press, 1975), p. 90.

But there are also sharp emotional differences between singles and doubles. For instance, only part of the reason doubles becomes more appealing to people as they grow older is physical. Aging also includes more of a readiness to bond and make alliances. As people pass into midlife, they're more in search of refinement and skill than they are of the raw power and high risk that characterized their earlier years. It is usually far easier for older people to put their destiny in someone else's hands, and what better description of doubles is there than that? Singles is a game of flashy, almost egotistical strokes; doubles requires that you sublimate your ego aspirations and "set up" your partner for a winning shot. If you're not willing to share the glory as well as the blame, you'll probably be better off on a singles court.

Jim is a typical doubles player, psychologically speaking. He's a thirty-nine-year-old department head in a major insurance firm, and he's been playing tennis for the past seven years. At the office he's always been considered a "company man" who's worked his way up from the sales force and plans to stay with the corporation for the rest of his career.

"I like to do things that require a lot of preparation and planning. Even when I was in sales, which gave me a great deal of freedom to work on my own, I enjoyed analyzing the attack I would use on a prospective client. But I always had two or three avenues to switch to if the first sales pitch didn't work. Now that I'm in management, I can combine this concept of thinking ahead with collective planning. I enjoy moving people around and figuring out solutions to complex personnel problems. I'd much rather plot the angles ahead of time than have to improvise at the last minute."

Not surprisingly, Jim is just the kind of player you'd like to have on your side of a tennis net. He's not likely to decide suddenly to free-lance, leaving you wondering where he is or what he's up to. He's a patient player, ready to "move people around" and "plot the angles." Best of all, he's willing to sacrifice himself for the good of the "company," which in tennis means hitting an unspectacular shot that sets up the other member of the team for the easy point.

Can we make any generalizations about the psychological makeup of the singles player versus that of the doubles player? Certainly it appears that most people have a strong preference for one game or the other. On the whole, singles players probably tend to be more independent, egotistical, competitive, dominant, and eager to take full responsibility. By contrast, doubles players tend to be older and lean more toward being dependent, social, gregarious and to some degree less willing to accept the total burden. Singles players don't bond as well as doubles players. (In Chapter 1 we discussed how bonding across the net in singles is bad for your game. It's a prerequisite in doubles, however, provided you limit it to your *own* side of the net.) But bonding can make such demands on self-esteem that doubles frequently becomes a tangle of emotions. The singles player who admits that he or she has no place in a doubles game is going to be happier than someone who persists at the four-cornered version despite every evidence that it is not emotionally suitable for him or her. We believe that doubles is the more "psychological" of the two games, beginning with the fact that you are now being scrutinized by six eyes instead of two. You know how disconcerting it is to see your opponents come together and whisper between points. "Oh, oh," you react. "I wonder what they've discovered about us." Hello self-consciousness, good-bye concentration.

For the moment let's deal primarily with "straight"—or nonmixed—doubles. Even in this game you're suddenly required to make decisions with regard to the opposition that are more complicated than those needed in singles. The main questions are: Which of the enemy do you want to hit to and who do you want to hit back at you? The answer would seem to be neither, since bonding across the net shouldn't even enter your mind; you should be trying to hit *away* from both your opponents, remember? Unfortunately, as we've seen, the unconscious notion of hitting *at* someone is difficult to overcome. So you select one opponent to "pick on," often choosing him or her regardless of the fact that the best available shot is not in that direction at all.

Which opponent do you single out? A computer would select the weaker of the two, but people are not always programmed so well. As in singles, your motives for certain actions may be based on hidden emotional factors. Perhaps your ego is such that you will go after the better player in order to prove to yourself that your down-the-alley backhand is nothing less than sensational. There you stand, bashing away straight ahead, much to the horror of a partner who knows full well that the best shot is clearly a delicate crosscourt lob. The boost to the self-esteem is so high when you finally *do* get one past that it overcomes any consideration you might have for winning points. If the player at whom you're aiming is stronger than you, so much the better; as we stated at the end of Chapter 5, an "Official Tennis Rule of Law" states that hitting with a superior opponent frequently enables you to play better yourself.

Further, you may not feel particularly comfortable aiming everything at the weaker player on an opposing team. It's not merely a matter of this tactic being "too easy." As in singles, you may be inhibited about being aggressive toward someone, whether it's because of his or her ineptness or because of your hidden feelings toward the particular person. Since doubles is thought to be more of an "attack game" than singles—with its leading premise being Those Who Control the Net Position Control the Game—players may be particularly reluctant to flail away at certain people while playing in a foursome. Sharp duels at the net, after all, are little short of just that: *duels.* (On the other hand, it's interesting to note that inhibition may frequently last only until a certain point, that point being the moment you begin to perceive that you might lose the match. Then, as with cheating, you may begin to search for a magical mystery cure. In this case, that can mean the sudden conviction that aggression is not such a bad thing after all.)

Still, the majority of doubles troubles are to be found on your own side of the net. Tennis players seem to sense the importance of making a good partnership. When a foursome arrives on the court it can turn the selection of teams into a discussion rivaling a summit conference for complexity. This happens even though there are only three possible combinations. Choosing a partner is considered akin in importance to choosing a wife or a husband. Indeed, many professional players have likened good tennis partnerships to good marriages. Unfortunately they neglect to consider the booming business being done in divorce courts.

But the analogy to mating is not inaccurate. Certainly, physical harmony is important, with the successful doubles team frequently being described in near-sexual terms. Players are told to work together as a duo, moving forward and backward together while shifting from side to side as a unit. It is generally believed that one of the partners should be the more aggressive of the two (or a "power" player), while the other should be satisfied with a more passive role (a "touch" player). But—again like sex—the union works best when emotionally as well as physically sound. According to Stan Smith and Bob Lutz, former United States doubles champions, "One player must, in the long haul, be slightly more offensive in his stroke making and attitude." [2] Smith and Lutz, it is assumed, are referring to the tennis court rather than the bedroom, but they could be talking about both.

What is "attitude"? Most tennis texts simply state that doubles partners must "get along" or "exhibit teamwork" and

[2] Stan Smith and Bob Lutz, with Larry Sheehan, *Modern Doubles* (New York: Atheneum, 1975), p. 105.

leave you to find your own definitions of the terms. Certainly, the concept of togetherness is difficult to contradict. Emotional compatibility is preferable to emotional combativeness. While equal technical ability isn't necessary, most tennis partnerships won't survive without emotional evenness. Beneath this nugget of accepted wisdom, however, lies a deeper desired psychological tennis fusion which is continually being thwarted by churned-up feelings.

Actually, many players embark on tennis as a hobby, believing that doubles is an emotionally easier game. Their theory is that having a cohort will reduce the strain of responsibility. "*We* lost," they feel, is easier to say than "*I* lost." But the emotional warmth to be gained by this type of thinking is usually offset by the cold realization that the player is now responsible for someone else. Suddenly the concern is not only about doing well but also about letting someone down. This can be an extremely heavy burden to bear, and it introduces a whole new layer of guilt. How many times have you seen a player who has muffed a shot in doubles reminding everyone within earshot that it's "*my* fault, *my* fault"?

Sharon, a twenty-four-year-old schoolteacher who is a tennis beginner, remembers the guilt of a recent doubles match.

"My partner that day was a fairly good player, certainly a lot better than I am. It made me a little nervous having her on my team, and wouldn't you know that I couldn't hit anything. I was terrible. In one game she got the ad point four straight times and I got us back down to deuce by missing my four service returns. And she was so patient with me! Which made me feel worse, of course. I felt so miserable that it got to the point where the only thing that would make me feel better would be when she made an error. That's right: I'd actually feel great when she missed a shot. It took the onus off me. Then it was I who was able to say, 'Don't worry' or 'Go get the next one.' And it was a lot nicer saying it than hearing it."

Often a doubles player will feel rejected by *all* the other players on the court. Being the weakest of four people is more humiliating than being the weaker of only two. All groups tend to create scapegoats, and a tennis foursome can be a particularly cruel world when one member is singled out. The less difference among its players' abilities the better. We know people who simply won't play doubles because they're afraid of the massive criticism—either real or imagined—it invites.

Let's look at what can begin to go wrong with a doubles partnership. Suppose two men (although it could just as easily be two women) walk onto the court to play together for the first time. Even before they begin, there is probably a bit of "new player anxiety." Each is slightly wary of the other, each hoping he has found a partner good enough to bolster his own self-esteem but not good enough to threaten him with humiliation. Tennis tensions are already bubbling. By the end of the first game—which is about how long it usually takes to discover these things—it is clear that one of the players is better than the other. This is hardly unusual and isn't in itself the cause of the doubles troubles ahead. It's what the players are about to *do* with this inequality that will cause an escalation of tennis tensions.

First, they may begin to lose. This causes problems because they both feel they shouldn't be falling behind these particular opponents. Each is experiencing a widening split between the actual self and the ideal self. As self-esteem continues to plummet with each lost point, aggression is released. Unfortunately it gets turned on the *partners* rather than on the other team. The stronger player begins to criticize his partner openly and decides to poach at every opportunity. He senses that the weaker player isn't trying and feels it's up to him to carry the whole load. In the meantime his partner realizes he's being criticized but feels his contribution is being undervalued. At first he feels ashamed, then resentful, then hostile. By now the team's aggression is hopelessly locked into its own side of the net. Open rivalry has broken out. Conditions reach the point where the stronger player also begins to muff his shots repeatedly. His rage has achieved a level where he is subconsciously "getting even" for the disappointment he believes his partner has caused him. The weaker player, meanwhile, is avenging himself by *really* giving up. The opposing team now needs only to go through the motions to win because our alleged "partnership" has long since disintegrated into two diametrically opposed individuals.

To borrow a question from a typical counseling manual: "Could this marriage have been saved?" Without a doubt. Back in Chapter 1 we warned that "tennis is a game of psychological sharing." The word *tennis*, we pointed out, comes from the French *tenez*, meaning "you take it." Doubles players must be particularly willing to put the emphasis on the *you*. This means altering their egos to allow their partners to "take" much of the action. For example, rather than trying to hit your first serve hard enough to penetrate a barn door, you should usually concentrate on placing it wide in the service box with spin so that the return will set up your partner at the net. This is easier said than done for many players who view themselves on the court as last bastions of the frontier of individualism.

Aggression between partners is the painful result of a sharp slash in the tire of self-esteem. But the tear can be quickly patched by partners who are willing and able to form that tight psychological fusion. Or to *bond*. As we mentioned, it's perfectly normal for one partner to be a stronger player than the other. Even beyond that, it is common—and frequently desirable—for one player to become the leader of the team, a kind of quarterback who provides inspiration and plans strategy. (In tournament play he or she is frequently and officially referred to as the "captain.") Problems don't occur until the players refuse to accept their differences. A bad partnership, as we have seen, is based on aggression and rivalry. A good one has a foundation of respect and tolerance. One disintegrates into hate, while the other—as corny as it may sound—blossoms into love. (Bravo! An instance where love *does* mean something in tennis.) Players won't physically coordinate their movements until they are psychologically coordinated. They won't rush the net together until there is an unspoken communication between them that it is time to get moving. They won't play as a unit until they think as a unit, and they won't think as a unit until both are willing to accept their different roles in something that is more than the sum of their individual parts. (Finding a player whose ability is equal to your own isn't a guaranteed way to avoid doubles troubles. Such partners sometimes then feel the need to compete with you instead of your opponents.)

Dave is a player for whom the discovery of a well-tuned partnership was a true revelation. He's a forty-one-year-old newspaper editor who's been playing tennis—much of it doubles—for about six years.

"For most of that time I had a series of partners and a series of mediocre games. It's not like I ever got in a fight with a partner or anything; it's just that, most of the time, it was like the two of us were playing singles on the same side of the net. If I was the better player, I tended to poach everything I could get near. If my partner was the better player, I felt left out. In the past year, though, I've had this particular partner who's much better than I am but with whom I play very well. Actually, I've stopped thinking in terms of myself playing well and started to think in terms of the team playing well. It's difficult to put the change into words. It's more than just teamwork. When things are going good it's almost psychic. I always know where he's going to be on the court, and I know my own limits. He covers more of the court and takes the lead—he even poaches a lot—but he does it in such a way that I don't feel like I'm not there. It's a very comfortable feeling, and it's put a whole new definition on the game as far as I'm concerned."

A word about poaching, which, strictly speaking, is the net person's lateral movement to intercept return of service. It has become something of a dirty word in tennis, and unfairly so. While it's true that some players do it too often, probably to satisfy exhibitionistic needs, others avoid it out of unconscious fear of being too aggressive toward their partners. Actually, poaching is a necessary part of the game, a weapon that can help prevent the other team from concentrating its attack on half the partnership. We believe more players should think in terms of becoming poachers because it will increase their aggressive involvement in the game—provided they don't poach unnecessarily or for reasons that have nothing to do with trying to achieve a solid balance.

One occasion when poaching is likely to be too prevalent is during mixed doubles. This form of the game is beginning to make waves in professional tennis as well as becoming an increasingly popular attraction at the hacker level as well. Yet many players are wary of it because they realize it introduces a complicating factor: the relationship between the sexes. As explained in Chapter 7, men and women tend to take on certain roles vis-à-vis each other on the tennis court. In general the male seeks the dominant position while the woman assumes the submissive posture. Whether this is right or wrong, it seems to be accepted at all levels of the game. Among the mixed doubles "commandments" of Bill Talbert, a champion doubles player and former Davis Cup captain, are warnings to women playing mixed doubles that they should "always let your partner appear to be boss" and "allow the man to serve first." Men are told: "Don't pick on the opposing lady unless you have to" and "When you're serving to the opposing woman, always use a slice or spin serve." [3]

Small wonder, then, that too much attempted poaching by the male partner often plagues mixed doubles. Although we

[3] Clark and Carole Graebner, with Kim Prince, *Mixed Doubles Tennis* (New York: McGraw-Hill, 1973), pp. 20–23.

know cases where the female member of a team has assumed the role of "captain," she more frequently acquiesces to the male. "I'm programmed to let him take over," one woman said to us during an interview. "I tend not to run as much when playing with a man who's eager to gallop about," another stated. "I defer to his ego."

Sandy, a young mother who plays in amateur doubles tournaments that are both mixed and otherwise, notices a sharp difference in her attitude when coupled with a man.

"With my female partner I'm clearly the aggressor on the team. I play the forehand court, and I really take charge. I know she—my partner—looks to me to be the leader and I like the role. But in mixed doubles the situation is entirely different. I'm aware that my partner is bigger than I am, for one thing. And he's more aggressive, too. So my game completely changes. Even though I consider myself to be a fairly aggressive person, I allow him to take over. He runs the show and, frankly, that's the way I like it. It's like being led around a dance floor."

Some men, though, become very inhibited when faced with the prospect of being aggressive *across* the net at a woman in mixed doubles. (Is this one reason why Talbert recommends a tender touch when serving to a woman?) While "targeting" of the woman opponent is common in professional tennis—money's at stake, after all—we've heard well-known pros deny the existence of such tactics with a straight face. This is probably partly an attempt to cope with guilt. Targeting is less frequent in "social tennis," where the desire to win is not enhanced by several thousand dollars. "It bothers me when I smash at the opposite sex" is the way one male player put it to us. "I'm simply less at ease when I smash at a woman," added a second. Thus, when offered an easy overhead at the net, it's not unusual for a male to let his inhibition get the best of him if there's a female form in the path of his shot.

Mixed doubles is a fertile breeding ground for the Uninvited Player-Coach and the Commander-in-Chief. Nowhere is this more true than in that most emotionally packed of all tennis combinations: mixed doubles in which the partners are husband and wife. Compared to the emotional static electricity of other forms of tennis, "married doubles" is often nothing short of lightning bolts. It can reach the heights of incivility in this most civilized game. Aggression untamed. "You couldn't get me on the same side of a tennis net with my husband for all the silver at Wimbledon," one woman told us. Of course, some couples enjoy playing together. "I know what to expect from my wife," another player said. "We're used to each other's style," is how a wife explained her choice to play with her husband as a partner, indicating that being familiar with someone's life style is helpful in appreciating his tennis style.

In contrast, some couples don't know when to quit. Their altar of worship is the notion of "togetherness." They insist on being partners *everywhere*, which means deciding to endure their private wars on the tennis court when a total disengagement is in order. Like John and Elizabeth, whose story began this chapter, many couples would be far happier if they called off their tennis union and allowed each member to go shopping for a new partner.

For many reasons people tend to play differently when partnered with their spouses. Marriage changes the game at all levels. Before marrying Clark Graebner, the former Carole Caldwell estimates that he handled about half the shots when they played top-ranked mixed doubles; after the marriage he took 70 percent of the shots.[4] On a nonprofessional level, one wife tells us, "If my husband hangs back, I hang back. That's what marriage is all about, isn't it?"

In both these cases certain aspects of the marriage situation are obviously affecting the game. That's what can make "mar-

[4] Ibid., p. 18.

ried doubles" so volatile: bringing facets of the marriage onto the court, particularly its problems. Here's what happened to Elaine, a thirty-two-year-old divorced salesperson whose mixed doubles became one more expression of her marriage difficulties.

"My husband and I were finally at the stage where we were seriously considering a separation. But we continued to play doubles together, for appearance's sake. I guess, though, we weren't fooling anybody. The gist of our problem was what happens to a lot of couples. He was spending more and more time away from home, and I felt he was ignoring me even when he was there. In fact tennis seemed to be the one place where we'd get to be together for more than five minutes. But things were just as bad on the court as off of it. I remember driving to one particular mixed doubles game—this one turned out to be a beaut—and listening to him tell me just to stay out of the way when the match began. We'd lost the last couple of times we'd played, and he was telling me that we would have won if I'd let him take more of the shots. What a load of crap. I told him he was already covering 80 percent of the court, so if he was so terrific how come we were losing? The fight didn't end in the clubhouse. As soon as we began to play, he began to act as if I wasn't there. He was cutting in front of me and poaching all over the place. After three games I quietly told him to let me into the game or I was going to walk off. 'Go ahead,' he said. And I did."

Such results are rare, but such emotions are not. The tennis court—where Elaine felt she was being ignored—had become an extension of the marriage. It happens all the time. We know one husband, a man who is particularly protective of his wife off the court, who goes to great lengths to poach when he's her tennis partner. It's his way of continuing to shield and protect her. Another player is distracted by what she is convinced are her husband's flirtations with female opponents. After parties she's been known to remark pointedly that he spent a half hour talking to another woman in the kitchen. Sometimes the on/off-court connection can be a bit odd. We're familiar with one couple who prefer to partici- pate in sexual "swinging"—that's the *off*-court behavior—and who also like to switch tennis partners as if the game were musical chairs.

There's a particular reason husbands and wives may make lousy tennis mates. They have a high emotional investment in one another. They're part of each other. The relationship is similar to that of parent and child: the parent has an ideal that he or she expects the child to live up to, and when the child can't do it, the parent shows disappointment, disapproval, and even contempt. When a wife misses an easy forehand volley, the husband feels as if *he's* missed it. When the husband dou- ble faults, the wife is no less angry than if she'd lost the point. Each expects the other to be perfect because each is a reflec- tion of the other's ideal self. That's why the Uninvited Player- Coach is such a prevalent specter in "married doubles."

It's also true that players feel more comfortable venting aggression and anger at their spouses than they do at ac- quaintances. With outsiders they may be all sweetness and light, but with their husbands or wives they turn into fire- breathing tennis dragons. "I criticize only my wife and no one else," one player emphasized to us. "You're nicer to someone you're not married to," a woman opined. Which is true. We tend to get angry more easily at people who have special meaning for us. Your emotional stake is higher when playing with your mate, and you also know exactly how much you can get away with. This is probably the reason many married couples team up despite the friction it generates.

In the end it may sometimes be best to do what John and Elizabeth did and sign up for a "tennis divorce." Some people play their best games when their spouses are among the enemy, thereby giving them license to let out smoldering aggression. It's merely a matter of putting your opponent in his or her place: *across* the net.

TEN WAYS TO NET PROFIT (for doubles players only)

1. *Be willing to admit that doubles might not be your game.* Playing in a foursome requires a different style than does playing singles and one that may not be suited to your psychological makeup. You might be too independent and competitive to accept a role in a partnership. If so, admit it and be happy with singles.

2. *On the other hand, "think doubles" as you grow older.* Psychologically speaking, most older people find comfort in alliances. They bond better. They enjoy subtlety more than they do power. Doubles satisfies these needs and produces a far less strenuous way to spend an hour than does singles.

3. *Play shots, not personalities.* You should try to select your shots solely on the basis of the tactical options available rather than aim them at a particular opponent. Although it does make sense to hit occasionally to the weaker player, trying to pick on someone can introduce problems that will only confuse your emotions and your game.

4. *Audition different partners.* Don't be afraid to spend some time searching for that elusive psychological tennis fusion. It won't come easily. Try to find a partner whose differences from yourself are acceptable to both of you and with whom you can think as a unit.

5. *Be supportive of a weaker partner.* "And now abideth Faith, Hope, Charity, these three; but the greatest of these is Charity." (Corinthians I: 13)

6. *Don't give up in the arms of a stronger partner.* Moping around the court because your partner is clearly better than you are can only be a detriment to your team. Accept his or her superiority. If possible, even let it flatter you.

7. *You can poach and still be a good egg.* While consistently covering more than your share of the court is something to avoid, too many players can't make up their minds whether to poach or not. Indecision is suicide in doubles. It is an "attack game," and the sooner you make up your mind to go to the offense, the more successful you'll be.

8. *Don't insist that your husband or wife always be your tennis partner.* Many couples have found that it is best to suspend their

union temporarily when they cross those little white lines. "Married doubles" is delightful when it works, but when it fails, it leads to more emotional drama than should ever be legally allowed on a tennis court.

9. *Don't bring your marriage onto the court.* Outside factors—even those you consider to be positive—interfere with your concentration. You and your spouse should make a conscious effort to leave your personal ups and downs in your respective locker rooms.

10. *Resist temptations to give orders and advice.* Doubles is filled with Uninvited Player-Coaches and Commanders-in-Chief. Few people hand out directions and opinions tactfully on the tennis court, and fewer can take them without feeling a rise in emotions. This is particularly true in "married doubles," where tennis tensions run particularly high.

9

Handling the Backhanded Psyche-out

Case study: BRUCE, age 44

Bruce began playing tennis a decade ago. He felt it would be the perfect game for him because it appeared to reward his apparent lack of emotion and strong sense of self-sufficiency. That was how Bruce viewed himself, and he was not alone in the assessment. As an only child, he had been left alone much of the time by parents who often gave the impression that they had better things to do than raise a son. Bruce, although hurt and distressed by this attitude, handled it by acting in much the same way toward others. He squelched his emotions wherever possible, treating friend and foe alike as faceless individuals.

Perhaps not surprisingly, he became an extremely successful businessman at an early age. He was viewed by competitors as a rock-solid manipulator who was never swayed by emotions when making a decision. While this led him to the top of the business community, it also created some problems in his marriage. He had married shortly after graduating from business college, choosing a well-bred bride as one might choose a race horse. But his discomfort with closeness led to a rather bleak union in which each partner eventually chose a separate path. Bruce's led first to sailing, an activity in which he was able to spend long hours alone on the water. Later he turned to tennis.

Bruce felt the key to good tennis was to treat opponents and partners as mere faceless individuals. "It's simply not an emotional game," he often argued, "at least not if you play it right." He viewed players who choke on the court as psychologically weak. He scoffed at the notion of being psyched out, at least as far as his own play was concerned. His coolness, he had always felt, would protect him from the likes of what we have termed tennis tensions.

Recently, however, an unusual incident occurred in one of Bruce's games. He was playing another top-flight businessman and an excellent tennis player as well. His opponent, using a smart chip-and-volley game, was leading 4–2 in the first set. The impending defeat, though, wasn't particularly crushing as the players got ready to begin the seventh game; Bruce was holding up his end and was clearly only a good shot or two away from pulling even. As the players split the first four points of the game, Bruce realized it was now or never. Then his opponent won the next point with a fine topspin lob. Bruce now had to win three straight points. He prepared to serve. And then, just before his toss, he heard the two words: "Break point!"

He hesitated. Something seemed to clutter his mind. Break point? Break point? An opponent had never said that before. Break point? What difference did it make? God, was it really break point? Bruce's first serve hit the net, halfway up. Certainly this guy doesn't seem to be someone who would say something like that, Bruce was thinking. Where did he get off saying that? What was going on here? The second serve hit the net on one bounce.

From that point on, Bruce's sudden retreat turned into a rout. His opponent ran out the set and won the second, 6–1. When he also took the first three games of the next set, it was he who suggested that they quit because it just did not seem to be Bruce's day. Bruce walked off the court, shaken. He realized that something had happened out there, that his mechanical defenses had broken down. Much later he returned to the image of that encounter with an awareness that it had been one of the first indications of a slow change in his life. Out of that loss—or actually out of that moment when but two words were uttered across a tennis net—came the realization that he was a vulnerable person and not the unflappable man he had always trained himself to be.

Whenever and wherever tennis enthusiasts get together off the court, discussion of the game they so revere frequently gets around to the fabled *psyche-out*. Someone always has a good first-person psyche-out tale to tell. How he was warming up for the finals of the Lower Punksawatanee Open when an offhand remark by his opponent turned his right arm into mint jelly. Or how the enemy lost track of the score during the Ladies' Day Four-Way Round Robin Ladder Cup Challenge Match Tournament and the storyteller couldn't remember how the devil to hit the ball from that moment on. When such trials are related, every tennis player within earshot nods sympathetically, solemnly, and knowingly. For the psyche-out, like cheating and choking, stalks the court in many recognizable forms.

First, a definition. You have been psyched out when the interaction between yourself and someone else on the court interrupts your integration and focus to the point that your play and/or pleasure are adversely affected. Translated, this means that something happens that triggers a temporary emotional conflict or sense of injury. A specific act causes your sense of being pulled together to be destroyed by self-consciousness, distraction, guilt, inhibition, or anxiety. Suddenly, you're at a psychological disadvantage. And the results are not good.

Second, a clarification. The psyche-out and the choke, although similar, are not the same thing. Tennis players may confuse the two terms, and understandably so, as the end result is equally distressing. The psyche-out is a triggered emotional imbalance in your game which causes you to stumble. The choke tends to be a more massive psychological inhibition which frequently results in a more damaging fall. The psyche-out tends to arrive from somewhere outside the psyche, while the choke is home-grown. (Usually, it's *"You psyched me out"* versus *"I choked."*) Players are frequently not sure when they've been psyched out, but most know a choke only too well when they meet it face to face. A psyche-out can happen at any time, while a choke tends to favor those critical moments "in the clutch." Finally, the psyche-out is probably the more common of the two

phenomena and usually lives a shorter life. But left un-
checked it can develop into the more severe helplessness of
the choke.

Much has been written making light of the psyche-out. Because it occurs as the result of a specific action, it is often
considered analogous to "gamesmanship" or "psychological
warfare." Gamesmanship became popular during the 1950s,
when its principles were set forth mainly by Stephen Potter, a
writer whose philosophy is best understood by the maxim "If
you can't volley, wear velvet socks." [1] "Psychological warfare"
is a more serious phrase, obviously taken from the military
and implying heinous results. Both, however, suggest *intent*,
which is obviously present when psychology is used as a
weapon in war or velvet socks are worn on a tennis court. The
psyche-out, however, is usually more accidental and unintended than not and may reflect the victim's vulnerability.
We are not talking here about lobbing into the sun or harass-
ing your opponent. The psyche-out is more subtle and less
deliberate than that, which is what makes it so difficult to spot
and often so impossible to cope with successfully.

The frequency of intentional psyche-outs—gamesmanship
or psychological warfare, if you will—tends to increase in
direct proportion to the stakes of the game. We have the impression that psyche-outs occur more often in tournament
tennis than in social tennis, and more on the professional level
than at the amateur level. At least they are more brilliantly
outlined. In 1975 Ilie Nastase was roundly criticized throughout the tennis world for "stealing" a match from fellow professional Ken Rosewall during the American Airlines Tournament in Tucson. He stalled and complained about calls to
the point where Rosewall's rhythm and concentration were so
destroyed that he was unable to play even passably. It was ev-

---

[1] Stephen Potter, *The Theory and Practice of Gamesmanship, or The Art of Winning Without Actually Cheating* (New York: Holt, Rinehart and Winston, 1948),
p. 24.

ident that the wily Nastase knew exactly what he was doing and that his behavior neatly fit Potter's definition of gamesmanship: "the art of winning games without actually cheating." The widespread outrage over the incident, though, indicates that most nonprofessional tennis players have little use for such blatant goings on, despite humorous books and articles to the contrary. To them gamesmanship *is* cheating.

But the unintentional psyche-out is something else again. Given the emotional level of tennis, it is almost unavoidable. We don't intend to tell you how to practice it on your opponent, because that would place it squarely in the realm of gamesmanship (though admittedly such a disclaimer is a bit like blueprinting the inner workings of a Molotov cocktail and expecting that no one will try to build one based on such a description). Instead, we'd like to approach the psyche-out from the point of view of helping you to recognize it when it is inflicted upon you. Pinpointing its existence *when it begins to happen to you* is more than half the battle of dealing with it. On the other hand, we might caution against the dangers of amateur psychology. Searching for a psyche-out to explain every lost set may be a convenient way of overlooking some very "unpsychological" drubbings.

Many players assume their opponents are too pure of heart to psyche them out. This is a mistake, since the opposition frequently isn't aware of what's happening either. A psyche-out can take place before, during, or after a game of tennis. The wording of an invitation to play can set off a psyche-out days before the match. There are few opportunities for *verbal* psyche-outs while the game is actually going on, as opposed to golf and billiards, two other games in which the psyche-out is prevalent. But between games come those spoken "passing shots" that flicker between opponents as they change ends of the court and provide enormous potential for emotional flare-ups. And since we've defined the psyche-out as being able to rob you of enjoyment as well as skill, a particular remark after a game has been completed can psyche you out of all the joy the play itself produced.

Who gets psyched out? No one is immune to the possibility of such inner crumbling, but certainly your emotional investment in the game may influence your capacity for loss of both skill and emotional stability. More importantly, different people are psyched out by different types of actions, words, or events. Your emotional history and current vulnerabilities are likely to be different from your partner's and are even likely to change from week to week, depending on the ebb and flow of your nontennis life. Within the game itself, a growing awareness of your opponent's superiority can produce an internal psychological avalanche. For simplicity's sake we've broken down potential psyche-out situations into four major categories you'll recognize easily by now: ritual, injustice, self-esteem, and aggression. Plus one relatively new one: sexuality. But remember that a particular circumstance could fall into more than one of these classifications, depending on how it affects an individual player.

The first category (ritual) is best illustrated by Mel, a fifty-four-year-old appliance-store owner who has played tennis once a week on the same day at the same time for the past five years.

"This is a crazy story, I'll tell you. I'm playing one of my salesmen for the first time not too long ago. We go out and hit a few to warm up, and I serve the first game, which I win at love. Then he takes the balls and gets ready to serve. For a second I almost yell at him because he's standing on the wrong side of the center line by a good two feet. I'm wondering if he really knows how to play this game after all. Just as I'm about to say something, he calmly steps to the deuce side of the line and serves. It's only an average serve, but I net the return. I walk over to the ad court and look up, and there he is on the deuce side! What in hell's going on, that's what I'm thinking now. But after he picks up the second ball, he stands there for a second or two and then—just like before—steps sideways as calm as you please into the right place and serves. This time I get it over the net, but not too strong. This keeps going on for a while. I mean, it looks to me like this is the way the guy serves, you know? Meanwhile, I'm mad as hell. But about the third game I'm sort of getting used to it. So what does he do? He stops doing it! Or he does it sometimes, and sometimes he doesn't do it. So I'm standing there wondering whether he's going to do it or not, I'm unsure of myself, and I can't return his serves worth a damn. I mean, it isn't illegal, but it sure is crazy."

Pity poor Mel, a typical tennis player tending to be on the obsessive/compulsive side. He wants everything to be in order with no ambiguity or uncertainty. Anything that stops the flow of the game—that breaks the *ritual*—will distract him and pysche him out. We know another player who got completely psyched out by the fact that his opponent held two balls in her hand for her second service instead of the customary one. He was so busy wondering about the presence of the extra ball that he was unable to concentrate on his return. The predictable result: into the net. Another player became disoriented when her male opponent continually returned her "out" serves as a form of practice. "You just don't *do* that," she complained, her concentration shattered.

The appearance of things "you just don't do" in tennis can cause further psyche-outs. Many players experience extreme discomfort when someone on their court (or even a neighboring court) lets loose with an outburst of anger. Notice the averted eyes and turned backs when this happens. Then there's the player who shows up in plaid Bermuda shorts and a Niagara Falls T-shirt, so altering the aura of the game as to induce a full-scale psyche-out in his opponent.

The devilish vagaries of tennis scoring can cause repeated nightmares for the player leaning toward obsessive/compulsive behavior. He or she must know the score at all times and will accept no substitutes. Uncertainty means trouble. It won't do any good to suggest "let's call it fifteen-all," because *that* would really destroy the ritual. Indecision is just not this person's favorite on-court circumstance. All that's needed to stir up difficulties is, say, an opponent who continually hesitates about making calls:

"Was that in or out?"

"Right."

"Right what?'

"Right, it was in or out."

"Aggghhh!"

Delays can also do the trick, as Nastase taught Rosewall. An opponent who checks the height of the net after every third game, wanders off to search for a ball that was lost last week, or receives a long-distance telephone call at break point can set one's teeth gnashing. And let some players be talked out of their expected and customary seven-minute warm-up before a match and their game disintegrates.

The second major category of psyche-outs involves the courts of justice—or perhaps we should say injustice. Tennis players tend to demand that a sense of fairness permeate the game; when they feel something unethical has encroached upon it they can become very anxious. Muriel, a forty-three-year-old mother who takes her tennis quite seriously, was recently involved in a game in which just such an episode took place.

"I was playing with my neighbor, a fairly good player whom I happened to be beating for once. It was my serve, halfway though the first set, when I noticed we were a ball short. I asked my neighbor about it and she just sort of flicked her head sideways toward the next court, on which there were two women playing. So I walked over there and asked if they'd picked up one of our balls by mistake, and they said no. I went up to the net on our court and asked my neighbor about the ball again. 'They've got it, all right,' she told me under her breath. 'I saw the tall one put it in her pocket.' Terrific, I thought. Just what we need in tennis: cops and robbers. So I trooped over and asked the tall one again, and she said no again.

Only she didn't check the bulge in her right-hand pocket. What the hell, I thought. If they want to act like jerks over a crummy tennis ball, that's all right with me. I shrugged at my partner and went back to the service line. I then proceeded to double fault three times in a row, which I don't think I've ever done in my life before."

Oh, the injustice of it all! To be seeded against a tournament's top player in the first round is enough to convince you that you have offended the tennis deities. To look across the net and see your opponent wearing a color-coordinated outfit, two-tone wrist band and leather glove while using one of those new oversized racquets can convince you that unfairness has signed on as your partner. To see his shots hit the net cord and bounce agonizingly onto your court is to sense that luck has sold you down the river. To watch an opponent play relentlessly to your under-the-weather backhand—even beyond the normal tendency to do so—is to become convinced that justice has closed her eyes to your cause. Anything that smacks of not being fair—from out-and-out cheating to phony excuses—can psyche out a player who carries a high sense of decency and righteousness onto the court. The conviction that he or she has been wronged saps the zing from shots and yanks the enjoyment from the game. This is supposed to be tennis, after all, not the roller derby.

And then there is self-esteem, the third breeding ground of the psyche-out. If it suddenly drops, watch your sense of self-worth dissipate and see your tennis tumble. Your opponent tells you he won't play very hard today because he's got an important match *tomorrow*. He asks, before you both walk onto the court, "Had those lessons yet?" He reminds you that you're ten years older than he is and accurately observes that you're still putting on weight. During the warm-up he suggests you straighten your arm on your backhand, and after the first game he remarks, "It's too bad your serve's off today." He announces the score more and more frequently as you fall further and further behind. Soon you swear he is actually calling some of your long shots "in." To add to this humiliation, he barely acknowledges your presence throughout the two sets and spends much of his time watching the activity two courts away. As you walk to the locker room he manages to comment that it's "too bad you've played so little this year."

Practically no one's self-esteem could survive *that*.

Doubles can be equally demoralizing. Always being teamed with the best player in a foursome conveys the none-too-subtle message that you are the worst player on the court. And how about overhearing someone say "Bad luck" to your teammate when he reveals that you're his partner for the upcoming club championship? There are a million ways you can be psyched out in tennis by being made to feel the fool, but it's important to remember that it's just as easy to take a sudden tumble if someone pumps your ego too high.

This is what happened to Julie. She's a mediocre "B" player, a thirty-four-year-old technical writer who's been playing tennis for several years. One day recently she got into a match that was over her head, and for a while she even played that way.

"Actually, I was only invited into this foursome as a last-minute substitute. The other three women are much better than I am, but I figured I had nothing to lose. And I don't know what it was, but I just began by playing very, very well. In fact, I was probably playing better than any of them. My partner and I won the first set, 6–3, and I was sky high. We took a break for a drink of water, and she mentioned how well I was playing. She said she'd seen me play recently and, boy, had I improved. Then one of the other women came over and asked me when I'd started taking secret lessons. Well, I want to tell you, these girls are good players and when they said stuff like that, it literally made my spine tingle. I couldn't wait to get back out there for the second set. I was ready to play all night. Unfortunately, it took only about half an hour for them to discover the truth. I went from the best to the worst so fast they must have thought I was playing with a different arm or something. We lost the next two sets, proving, I guess, that a leopard can't change its spots."

We've already seen why things like this happen: worries about being envied, fears of causing humiliation, and a sense that achieving a great height can only lead to a great fall. It's not merely a matter of monstrous overconfidence. Julie sounds like she backed off when faced with the realization she would have to live up to her stunning performance in the future. We know many other players who experienced sudden ego uplifts only to have them turn into equally sudden emotional downfalls. It can even be a casual remark—perhaps about how well you're looking these days—that causes your cup of self-esteem to run over. We're acquainted with one player who was licked in a match before it started, beaten by the sudden emotional stroking his opponent gave him in the locker room. It covered everything from his new tennis bag to his wife's appearance. Another player—when an opponent went into a fit of self-criticism—began to feel so good about his own playing that he lost five straight games before he woke up to what was happening. A particularly subtle example of this type of behavior can be seen when a player sends a "sitter" toward you at the net and bellows the standard "Oh, no!"—the implication being that with your unwavering ability the point is as good as over. Which it is, but frequently not in your favor.

The fourth class of psyche-out involves aggression. As with self-esteem, there are two types of situations that are likely to make you anxious. The first—and less common—occurs when there are suggestions that you're not the aggressive type and should perhaps be spending your time elsewhere. "Gee, you do so well for someone who doesn't hit very hard," you're told. "What a cute little racquet, dear," someone adds. "How on earth do you get the ball over the net?" Things like that. Perhaps your partner suggests you're not trying. (In married doubles this is frequently more than a suggestion.) Or maybe the receiver moves so close to the net on your service that it looks as if he or she is about to leap over it. Such goings on can leave you temporarily wondering if perhaps you haven't wandered into the wrong game. Certainly, they can make you feel inadequate.

But it is the other side of the aggressive coin that causes far more psyche-outs: guilt over too *much* aggression, whether real or imagined. A perfect example of this is what happened to Gerry, a doctor and a strong player who is used to tournament competition.

"The guy I was playing this one day is only fair, and to be perfectly honest I can't remember the last time I lost to him. Correction: I've never lost to him, and it's only been close, oh, maybe two or three times. He's kind of an awkward player who stays back at the baseline, but he's a real plugger and a lot of fun to play with. He gets a real kick out of the game. So we were playing on this one Saturday, and I was pretty far ahead in the first set when he hit a kind of short, weak shot. I moved in on it, and all of a sudden out of the corner of my eye I saw him coming to the net. Now this guy never came to the net in his life before, at least not that I know of, and all of a sudden he's all arms and legs and headed right at me. And on a short ball! Well, it was an easy passing shot for me, so I hauled it off and hit the hell out of it. I'll never forget the look on his face—it seems funny now but it didn't then—as the ball came at him. With his coordination he didn't have a prayer of getting out of the way, and it caught him square on the cheek, right under his glasses. They went one way, he went the other, and I think his legs went somewhere else. Now I'm a doctor, and as soon as I got to where he was sitting, I could see that he wasn't really hurt, just kind of startled. And so was I. For a second it had looked like the ball was going to tear his head off. He insisted on finishing the set, and thank God he decided to stay away from the net. But it really affected my game. Now I felt sorry for him, because I didn't want to hit the ball hard anymore. My shots were flat. I think I eventually won by only about 6–4."

Injuries and awkwardness aren't the only things that can inhibit your aggression. Often a subtle comment can be the cause. An opponent might suggest that he's really no match for you, or perhaps even call you a "killer." [2] He may suggest that you take it easy on him because he hasn't played in several weeks. Or perhaps he or she will choke on the court, causing you subconsciously to feel guilty and pull in your weaponry. It is within this field of inhibited aggression that the psyche-out is closest to the choke.

The final source of the psyche-out revolves around matters of sexuality. Yes: sex in tennis. Is it a sexual game? Certainly it can be sensuous on the surface—graceful and fluid motions are carried out by skimpily clad men and women whose vocabulary of words such as "stroking" and "balls" leads to all sorts of double entendres. On the other hand, tennis has its image to live up to. Notwithstanding its increasing tendencies toward an après-tennis scene, the game is perceived by most of its players as being properly asexual. It is viewed as pristine and above board. The truth is probably somewhere in between. In the broad definition of the term, tennis *does* have sexual overtones, probably more than are imagined by most of its players. And yet sexuality—a dominant American theme when good friends get together, as it were—is denied its role on the court. It is traditionally hidden or repressed under a cloak of respectability. As a result anything that tends to sexualize the game openly will disturb it, in much the same way a break in the ritual causes discomfort.

[2] There is a whole warlike and violent vocabulary to tennis, as there is to all sports. But to some ears it sounds *more* violent and warlike. "Killer," "masher," "powerhouse," "butcher," and "cutthroat" are a few of the labels tossed about. No wonder people are inhibited.

Something that happened to JoAnn illustrates this perfectly. She is a thirty-one-year-old architect who joined a female friend in a recent mixed doubles match with two of the
friend's male acquaintances.

"Let me begin this story by saying that, to me, tennis is tennis.
I'm not into all this socializing that goes on. I go to the club, I play, I
go home. I've been playing since I was fourteen, and I take the
game seriously. That's why I usually don't get into games with people I don't know, but in this case I let my friend talk me into it. So
we met these two guys at the club. First of all I felt like I was being
inspected. They spent all this time deciding who was going to be
whose partner, with a few juvenile lines about who'd stay with whom
'afterwards.' Well, that's all right, so long as it stops when the game
starts. But it didn't stop, at least not with this guy who ended up as
my partner. We began playing, and the first thing I noticed was that
we had to have a discussion every third point or so. And that he had
to put his arm on my shoulder. And that he had to put on his best
leer. In the second game I went up to play net while he served and
what do I hear? Something about 'the view being great from back
here.' Now, really, do I need that? I've got enough problems out
there without thinking about some joker getting off by looking at
my ass. Try thinking about that while you're trying to concentrate
on the game at the same time. I played lousy after that, really lousy,
and when we were finished I couldn't get out of there fast enough.
Alone."

JoAnn's concentration was broken by the sexuality she perceived as being directed toward her. But it can also happen
when *you're* the voyeur, distracting you to the point of uneasiness and guilt. Physical contact of any type—whether during
play or between games at the net—can make certain players
uneasy if not outright anxious, particularly if they have deep
concerns about their sexual identity. (Actually, the spark may
only be innuendo.) And sexual exhibitionism, appearing in a
game as prudish as tennis, can knot the straight laces of many
a player. In general, if sexuality remains repressed there is

less chance that tennis tensions will creep in. But if it surfaces, the psyche-out will probably not be far behind—leaving the puzzled victim with another mysterious story about tennis instability to tell his or her friends with a shaking head.

FIVE WAYS TO NET PROFIT

1. *Alert yourself to possible unintended psyche-outs.* Don't think you're invulnerable, because no one is. The potential psyche-out lurks inside every opponent or partner, and expecting yourself to be protected by someone else's purity is naïve.

2. *Examine your emotions.* Different players are vulnerable to different types of psyche-outs. Are you the well-ordered type? Feel cheated a lot? Think you're tops? Concerned about hurting others? Easily flustered by sexuality? If you find you're being frequently psyched out, you've got some questions to ask yourself.

3. *If you feel an opponent is psyching you out, don't be afraid to say so.* Too many players trundle through games vaguely aware that they're being bothered by an opponent but afraid to do anything about it. Speak up. Get the air cleared. He or she will probably be surprised at what you say and will be willing to make a few changes. If not, you may want to find someone else to play with.

4. *Don't blame defeat on a higher power.* An awful lot of players get psyched out by thinking they're being beaten by the tennis gods. Wrong. They're being beaten by (a) the person or persons on the other side of the net or (b) themselves. God is not a tennis player.

5. *Beware of courtship on the courts.* Yes, sex exists in tennis. On rare occasions it can actually spur you on to greater heights. In some areas the sport is even becoming an updated version of the great American dating bar. On the whole, however, dwelling on the anatomy only interferes with concentration and creates distractions. Keep your eye, as they say, on the ball.

10

Decalogue: A Psychological Value System

"Linesmen ready? Ballboys ready? Play!"

Few of us ever reach the point where we enjoy the luxury of a referee sitting at courtside informing us that the moment of truth is at hand. That is the lot of professionals or tournament-toughened amateurs. Yet for hacker and pro alike there is the final realization that we must indeed "Play!"—that all the anxiety and chitchat and warm-up and brouhaha are finally over and that we must start hitting tennis balls in something approaching competitive fashion. As we have seen, there are not many who pass through such moments without at least an emotional twinge or two.

But despite what you may have deduced so far, it *is* possible to have more fun playing tennis than many people currently seem to have. And we're not just talking about those rare and euphoric moments when you are transported to tennis heaven by hitting the "perfect" shot. Instead, it may be possible to reevaluate and modify your psychological value system on the court. If successful, this could limit—and in some cases even eliminate—much of the emotional jamming that may be interfering with your enjoyment of the game.

Does that mean you'll necessarily play better? There you go again: looking for magical cures. Yet there may be more than a bit of truth to the cliché that "happy tennis players are better tennis players." We acknowledge that there are some players for whom the pain of the game has special meaning and priority—and that this may even be the major reason for their attachment to it. When we talk about increasing "enjoyment" of the game, we don't suggest turning it into a raucous contest of giddiness and laughter that would cause the venerable Major Wingfield to wonder what he wrought when he loosed modern tennis on the world a century ago. What we mean is imbuing your tennis with more personal satisfaction and a sense of worth by clarifying and minimizing the emotional hang-ups that continually nip at its heels. And we can predict with some certainty that when many of these "problems" are reduced, the result will be an improved game.

So here we offer a Decalogue, a sort of Ten Commandments aimed at helping achieve what might be called "pleasure tennis." We have touched upon or alluded to some of these points earlier, but they're so central to balancing love and hate on the tennis court that they should be reiterated, expanded upon, and carved into memory. They are an attempt to pull together many of the observations made earlier about ritual, bonding, aggression, self-esteem, anxiety, guilt, and inhibition. Regular attention paid to these psychological issues can be the key that finally reduces tennis tensions and allows one to "Play!" in the truest and most enjoyable sense of the word.

1. Remember you're not alone.

We don't want to leave the impression that only disturbed or even particularly sensitive people respond emotionally to the vagaries of tennis. Too many of the thirty-odd million players running around America's tennis courts see themselves as literal "tennis nuts" while viewing opponents or partners as marvels of modern machinery who are able to turn out groundstrokes without the slightest interference from the nervous system.

Admittedly there are many people who are disturbed but whose tennis games are models of cool and deliberate concentration while their lives are in turmoil. For them the tennis court is a haven of control and peace: everything fits into place, and they're at their best. Others are cool both on and off the court. Most players, however, suffer from tennis tensions to one degree or another. Inside each of them boils a caldron of emotions which eventually bubbles over in varying amounts. Unfortunately, there is a tendency to look upon other players as being particularly unflappable, an inclination that often leads to treating them as unbeatable. Which, of course, they're not.

It's the rare person who can keep his or her psychological distance from other people while playing. Bruce, whose case study is found at the beginning of Chapter 9, thought tennis wasn't an emotional game "if you play it right." But when an opponent unexpectedly reminded him that he was facing break point, machinelike Bruce broke down. Few people who have more than casually hit a tennis ball have been without tennis tensions. That apparently cool and collected customer across the net has undoubtedly brought his or her share of turmoil to the court as well.

Perhaps the tendency to distort a merely competent adversary into an invulnerable tennis computer—particularly when you're losing badly—is advanced by books and those instructors who emphasize the rare skill of conscious concentration. They conjure up single-minded automatons who possess the anticipation, timing, and proper stroke to put the ball wherever they want while paying no heed to the psychological needs of their opponents or themselves. But it's a myth that most tennis players achieve this ideal all the time. And you're making a mistake in believing you're a "nut" if you can't constantly live up to it yourself.

2. Find the proper frame of mind.

Regardless of the proclivity for tennis tensions, we don't want to suggest that you can't strive to reduce them. It's just that conscious concentration is really not the best attitude to assume toward the game.

You know, for example, that there is simply not enough time when hitting a tennis ball to analyze all the physical movements of the shot from preparation to followthrough. The ball zips past you before you can even tell yourself, "Racquet back!" It is therefore best hit without self-consciousness. It must be stroked on the basis of experience and usually follows a unique pattern for every player. Intellectual attempts to evaluate the mechanics of every shot lead to disruption. Instead the player must stroke "thought-lessly," working in an easy flow.

In much the same way, *emotional* interference should also be reduced. Conscious concentration implies a concerted collection of data, and we would suggest that a suspension of deliberation is more in order. As we have said before, proper integration is achieved by minimizing and containing all those extraneous emotional issues and conflicts that get in the way—issues centering around ritualization, self-esteem, and aggression, for instance.

Maintaining the proper frame of mind means playing almost without thought. In the same way the player shouldn't get caught up in the minutiae of his backhand technique, neither should he be ruminating—subconsciously or not—about whether or not he really wants to smash the daylights out of the woman across the net. In this optimal state, the ego does not make outrageous demands. Instead, the player operates on a kind of higher plane where emotional judgments, self-criticism, and punishment are lessened.

One way of approaching this frame of mind and of reducing self-consciousness is to focus on what you *want* to happen rather than on what you're doing wrong. You can also, when playing doubles, overcome mild choking and other emotional ailments by using your partner. Allow him or her to take over some of your direction—pointing out where you might place your serve, discussing whether or not you should move to the net, and generally proposing other forms of strategy. Acknowledging such suggestions can aid anticipation, increase bonding, and help avoid some of the more impossible demands you might be prone to make yourself.

It is no accident that the world's best tennis players claim to have moments when nothing penetrates their minds. They even have a word for this state, though they are hard put to describe its symptoms. They call it being in the "Zone," the term having been taken from a science fiction television show of the 1960s entitled "Twilight Zone." Yet the "Zone" is neither science nor fiction. It comes from the reduction of emotional clutter.

3. Realize it's only a game.

There's a confusing irony to tennis. On the one hand, the game is clearly play, an elaborate reliving of early childhood moments of give-and-take and catch-and-toss. On the other hand, it is obviously a serious arena where many ambivalent life situations are duplicated and where many "real-life" emotions such as love and hate turn up. So which is it? Mere child's play or life itself? Or a combination of both?

The answer is *both*, because tennis, like early play, is a chance to *play at life*. As we've seen again and again, it contains many of the same themes that run through the psyches of all of us. It is a kind of miniature stage where situations are acted out without any of the real consequences found in the "outside world." In one sense, as we suggested earlier, it's like a television soap opera: it has a plot, a conflict, and a conclusion. And like this same television drama, it *isn't real:* all the actors (players) leave the stage (court) at the end of the performance (match) and go home to their lives untouched by the events of the hour.

But problems arise when the actors don't realize that they're acting. The lines between what's real and what isn't become blurred. The performance turns into something more than a show. Tennis situations become more than symbols of skill and are often treated with a solemnity that would do justice to issues of life and death. For that is what tennis has become to more than a few of its players—a matter of life and death. They've forgotten that they're on stage, and their emotional investment overwhelms their sense of play. They are taking the game too seriously and acting as if survival itself is at stake.

To begin to achieve the proper frame of mind described in our second commandment, you've got to get back to treating tennis as *play,* as a *game.* One of the ways to deflect emotional interferences is to realize that you are not involved in a holy crusade when you walk onto a tennis court but are merely about to perform a pleasant social ritual in a reasonable facsimile of the real world. The play's the thing, after all.

4. Follow the best policy: reality.

As we've pointed out, tennis players tend to be egotists of the highest order. They invariably think they are better shot makers than they really are. Listen to the inner dialogues: "You shouldn't have missed that one!" or "Why is it I never play as well as I should?" (It's interesting that the inner dialogue is almost always damning, never praising.) Their ideal selves are soaring somewhere up in the clouds, but their actual selves are constantly bringing them down to earth with an unhappy thud. They imagine they are capable of playing at an illusionary upper level somewhere, from which the inevitable fall is only that much more painful. Overexpectation = overcriticism = tennis tensions.

In truth, however, a ten-year "veteran" of the game would be considered a novice were tennis his or her occupation. Let's say, for instance, that you play twice a week for a total of two hours. That's 104 hours in one year, or the equal of a little more than two and one-half 40-hour work weeks. In ten years this represents only about six months spent on the tennis court on a Monday-to-Friday, nine-to-five "work" basis. Six months! How good an architect would you be after only six months of study? How good a plumber six months after picking up your first wrench? Yet tennis players with the same amount of training remain convinced they are capable of miraculous feats.

There is something else players are rarely likely to admit: namely, that their game has "peaked" after several years. They don't realize they're not going to get any better unless they substantially increase their playing time. Instead of admitting this, however, they cling to the dream that they will improve forever, with the inevitable result being on-court frustration and anguish.

One of the best ways to deflect subconscious emotional interference from your tennis game is to take a less exaggerated look at your abilities and potential. Simply try to bring your ideal self and your actual self closer together. This is not to suggest that you shouldn't have goals, but only to say that they should be realistic ones. Shortening the distance between reality and fantasy is one of the easiest ways to get a grip on tennis tensions.

5. Balance your aggression.

Aggression—and how you deal with it—may not only be the most important emotional factor in your tennis. According to our observations, it may also be the single most important reason why people quit the game. They feel uncomfortable, annoyed, or even bored on the court by the antagonism sensed in "play." Some people are just unable to mobilize aggressive energy. Aggression appears to be the single psychological area that most affects the actual *play*—as opposed to the *pleasure*—of the game.

Overaggressors rarely present low profiles: they try to smash the ball too often or may break out in racquet-hurling tantrums. Underaggressors are more difficult to spot, though there are probably more of them. They keep their discomfort to themselves. They might be seen consistently retreating to the baseline, for instance, or choking on the taste of approaching victory.

While occasional outbursts of anger on the tennis court might be good release mechanisms for certain people, the guilt often associated with them usually outweighs any of their benefits. At the same time, however, the pent-up aggression of daily life can be channeled into the actual game with positive results. Turned loose within the safe limitations of the sport, aggression in tennis takes place in one of the few arenas where the average person can be a guiltless attacker. But many people are uneasy about giving themselves such permission, not realizing that inhibition often poses a bigger threat to skill and pleasure than open rage.

Perhaps you should look at aggression this way: there may be days when you tend to hit the ball into the net, and there may be others when you're inclined to hit long. What you're after is something in the middle—over the net, but not out of the court. Aggression, too, has to travel a certain distance—but not too far. You must be willing to release enough to play the game effectively, while at the same time making sure you keep it within the sport's limits. Like a tennis shot itself, aggression requires a delicate balance between too soft and too hard.

6. Recognize your opponent's "emotional mistakes."

Tennis players are forever hearing that theirs is a "game of mistakes." (Just as golfers, football players, and probably even Japanese sumo wrestlers are told the same thing about *their* sports.) He who makes the fewest errors, the old story goes, usually wins the match. And who can argue with that, even though it says nothing about a player actually forcing those mistakes to happen? Our only quarrel with this notion is that it obviously refers only to the likes of erratic shots or poor strategy. We think that tennis is replete with "emotional mistakes," too, and that it is the smart player who ignores or even goes so far as to take advantage of those that turn up on the other side of the net.

An opponent who continually sputters inner dialogues, for instance, should not be allowed to make you feel that you are inflicting harm. A player whose ideal self demands that he or she attempt only spectacular high-risk shots that lose points need not be discouraged from such a plan. And an opponent who doesn't have his or her aggressiveness operating is probably ripe for a full-scale frontal assault.

But many tennis players are unable to take advantage of their opponents' emotional mistakes because they are so hung up on their own problems. This is an amazingly easy state in which to find yourself. You become so wrapped up in self-assessment that you completely forget there is someone on the other side of the net whom you should be observing and trying to beat. Remember that your *real human opponent* is over there. There are likely to be times when it's best not to try harder yourself, but to let him or her make some of the psychological errors. Don't be afraid to make use of them.

7. Expect injustice on the courts.

Players often believe—perhaps because they find themselves on a "court"—that justice should triumph. But tennis, like life, turns out to be a mixed bag of rights and wrongs. Expecting it to be the pure game its whiteness so openly promises is another way of widening the distance between the actual and the ideal.

This is more than a matter of failing to expect others to cheat a bit, though that is part of the problem. Some players react to cheating badly because they are simply not prepared for it. Tennis has had such an angelic glow that the thought of satanic behavior is impossible for many players to cope with. The resultant sense of hurt is enormously demoralizing.

But beyond this there is a broader type of sensed unfairness, one that is more commonly experienced. It surfaces, for example, when a well-stroked shot hits the net cord and bounces back or when an opponent's desperate lunge results in a fluky winner. These are the moments when tennis players resort to all types of scapegoats, from luck to destiny to the gods.

The belief there is a higher power that somehow determines your tennis ability may cause the same feeling of injury that frequently accompanies the suspicion you've been cheated. This wouldn't be of concern if players were able to channel their hurt into the game in the form of aggression, but unfortunately the anger and frustration that frequently result get turned upon the self. This leads to (1) a rage of protest during which shots are smashed with vengeance or (2) a deadening of the game which is interrupted only by a muttered inner dialogue.

To help avoid such complications, expect some moments of unfairness or bad luck when you play. When they occur, remember that "tennis court" may well be a contradiction of terms.

8. Muzzle your inner and outer dialogues.

By now you should understand that flare-ups of tennis tensions can be caused by what is said or implied on the court, as well as by what happens. But outright verbal confrontations are rare. Psyche-outs are the frequent result of casual comments made without malice in a game in which there is constant pressure to socialize. They sometimes take place between games or between points. Depending on his or her vulnerabilities, a player's game can be struck down by a seemingly harmless remark intended to do no more than fill a verbal void. It seems that the pioneers of tennis knew what they were doing when they created a game characterized by hushed tones and little conversation. Today's tennis players would do well to follow their lead.

While the effect of your inner dialogue is relatively harmless to you and can even be helpful (at worst, it is more symptom than disease), it can certainly disrupt opponents and partners. Moaning and groaning has never been known to help a tennis ball fly over a net. There are plenty of instances on record where players with such tendencies have suddenly found that their presence on the tennis court is no longer requested with quite the same frequency it once was. Few like to be forced to listen to the morose masochism of a constant complainer.

As for remarks aimed at others, they, too, should in all probability be limited. Obviously, doubles teams must hold occasional strategy conferences. And complimenting an opponent's good shot is certainly considered *de rigueur*. But the potential for lighting the spark that will set off tennis tensions is extremely high when words start flying around the court. We're aware of too many incidents where a cutting remark—sometimes intentional, more frequently not—has opened up a wound that has festered for several sets. Since there's no way to predict fully a particular player's vulnerability to various comments, you are better off saying nothing in the first place.

Actually there are some individuals who, in a complete turnabout, are able to practice and develop a *positive* inner dialogue on the court—or at least one in which encouraging comments help remedy the usual imbalance. Gentle advice to relax frequently provides low-key inspiration. In time it can even help you break a slump by focusing your aggression toward the net. Which, of course, is where it belongs.

9. Limit your psychologizing.

There's a certain danger in dealing with your tennis emotions. Just as a player can be psyched *out,* so can he or she be psyched *in.* By that we mean there is a tendency to lose your sense of proportion on the court and to start thinking that to master tennis you must only master your emotions. It is well to remember that everything that happens in the game is not "psychological." Fatigue, overeating, accident, and just plain luck influence the outcome of many matches. When one hasn't lived up to expectations—win or lose—it's almost too easy to blame a bad day at the office. The truth may be that you simply aren't spending enough time on the court.

Skill and practice shouldn't be overlooked. Tennis is a strenuous game which demands an incredible amount of physical ability in order to be played well. (Aren't you struck by the fact that you rarely see any good tennis players who are overweight?) And yet there are still people who come to the game determined to get by on some sort of innate ability which they imagine to be lurking within their omnipotent selves. They eschew lessons and instruction and may be further encouraged in this approach when someone tells them the game is a "psychological" one.

Mastering all the other points in this Decalogue will mean very little to you if you refuse to let yourself learn. Maintaining a realistic self-image, for instance, will do you no good if you cannot hit the ball over the net. Maximizing your aggression within the game's boundaries will be of little use if you don't understand the proper time to move to the net. Emotional balance is only one side of the tennis pyramid. The structure simply won't stand without the other two: skill and practice.

10. Watch the games people play.

Nothing gets you revved up for tennis quite like watching a couple of professionals go at the game tooth and nail. Their grace and coordination are completely seductive as they glide about, their speed and power awesome as they hammer away at one another. You marvel at these skills as they are displayed on the court, and you leave the stadium shaking your head at the display you have witnessed.

But what, exactly, have you seen? Probably you have looked for many of the subtle things you're supposed to look for when watching the pros play: whether the server is changing pace, whether the receiver is giving away his intentions, or whether one of the players is consistently hitting short of the baseline. Things like that. But how about looking at a match from a different point of view? Why not try to spot the visible emotional factors that can give you a whole new perspective on the game you're watching? Actually, you don't have to limit such viewing to professionals. In fact, it's probably better if you don't. Watch *anybody* play, but use the new criteria you've learned. . . .

Are the players relying heavily on ritual? Are they playing in predictable patterns? Are they bonding? Are inner dialogues being sputtered? Are players trying to kill the ball? Hanging at the baseline? Exploding into rage? Watching other players? Watching *you?* Being less than honest? Choking in the clutch? Forming antagonistic doubles partnerships? Undermining their own games?

There's a great deal to be learned, emotionally as well as physically, from watching other people play tennis. True, much of what is going on is invisible to the player as well as to the viewer. But many clues to the state of the psyche can be seen bubbling to the surface. Picking them out in others not only helps you find them in your own tennis game, but also makes life on the courts more enriching, satisfying, and enjoyable.

Play!